CRIMINAL
INVESTIGATIONS

CELEBRITIES AND CRIME

CRIMINAL INVESTIGATIONS

CRIMINAL
INVESTIGATIONS

CELEBRITIES AND CRIME

MICHAEL NEWTON

Consulting Editor: **JOHN L. FRENCH**,

CRIME SCENE SUPERVISOR,
BALTIMORE POLICE CRIME LABORATORY

CHELSEA HOUSE
P U B L I S H E R S

An imprint of Infobase Publishing

CRIMINAL INVESTIGATIONS: Celebrities and Crime

Chelsea House
An imprint of Infobase Publishing
132 West 31st Street
New York NY 10001

Library of Congress Cataloging-in-Publication Data
Newton, Michael, 1951-
Celebrities and crime / Michael Newton ; consulting editor, John L. French.
p. cm. — (Criminal investigations)
Includes bibliographical references and index.
ISBN-13: 978-0-7910-9402-0 (alk. paper)
ISBN-10: 0-7910-9402-2 (alk. paper)
1. Crime—United States—Case studies. 2. Criminals—United States—Case studies. 3. Murder—Investigation—Case studies. 4. Celebrities United States—Case studies. 5. Celebrities—Crimes against—United States. I. French, John L. II. Title. III. Series.
HV6250.4.C34N49 2008   364.10973—dc22
2008009482

Text design by Erika K. Arroyo
Cover design by Ben Peterson

Cover: Metal garage door mural emblazoned with Tupac Shakur's likeness.

Printed in the United States of America

Bang EJB 10 9 8 7 6 5 4 3 2 1

This book is printed on acid-free paper.

All links and Web addresses were checked and verified to be correct at the time of publication. Because of the dynamic nature of the Web, some addresses and links may have changed since publication and may no longer be valid.

Contents

Foreword

In 2000 there were 15,000 murders in the United States. During that same year about a half million people were assaulted, 1.1 million cars were stolen, 400,000 robberies took place, and more than 2 million homes and businesses were broken into. All told, in the last year of the twentieth century, there were more than 11 million crimes committed in this country.*

In 2000 the population of the United States was approximately 280 million people. If each of the above crimes happened to a separate person, only 4 percent of the country would have been directly affected. Yet everyone is in some way affected by crime. Taxes pay patrolmen, detectives, and scientists to investigate it, lawyers and judges to prosecute it, and correctional officers to watch over those convicted of committing it. Crimes against businesses cause prices to rise as their owners pass on the cost of theft and security measures installed to prevent future losses. Tourism in cities, and the money it brings in, may rise and fall in part due to stories about crime in their streets. And every time someone is shot, stabbed, beaten, or assaulted, or when someone is jailed for having committed such a crime, not only they suffer but so may their friends, family, and loved ones. Crime affects everyone.

It is the job of the police to investigate crime with the purpose of putting the bad guys in jail and keeping them there, hoping thereby to punish past crimes and discourage new ones. To accomplish this a police officer has to be many things: dedicated, brave, smart, honest, and imaginative. Luck helps, but it's not required. And there's one more virtue that should be associated with law enforcement. A good police officer is patient.

Patience is a virtue in crime fighting because police officers and detectives know something that most criminals don't. It's not a secret, but most lawbreakers don't learn it until it is too late. Criminals who make money robbing people, breaking into houses, or stealing cars; who live by dealing drugs or committing murder; who spend their days on the wrong side of the law, or commit any other crimes, must remember this: a criminal has to get away with every crime he or she commits. However, to get criminals off the street and put them behind bars, the police only have to catch a criminal once.

The methods by which police catch criminals are varied. Some are as old as recorded history and others are so new that they have yet to be tested in court. One of the first stories in the Bible is of murder, when Cain killed his brother Abel (Genesis 4:1–16). With few suspects to consider and an omniscient detective, this was an easy crime to solve. However, much later in that same work, a young man named Daniel steps in when a woman is accused of an immoral act by two elders (Daniel 13:1–63). By using the standard police practice of separating the witnesses before questioning them, he is able to arrive at the truth of the matter.

From the time of the Bible to almost present day, police investigations did not progress much further than questioning witnesses and searching the crime scene for obvious clues as to a criminal's identity. It was not until the late 1800s that science began to be employed. In 1879 the French began to use physical measurements and later photography to identify repeat offenders. In the same year a Scottish missionary in Japan used a handprint found on a wall to exonerate a man accused of theft. In 1892 a bloody fingerprint led Argentine police to charge and convict a mother of killing her children, and by 1905 Scotland Yard had convicted several criminals thanks to this new science.

Progress continued. By the 1920s scientists were using blood analysis to determine if recovered stains were from the victim or suspect, and the new field of firearms examination helped link bullets to the guns that fired them.

Nowadays, things are even harder on criminals, when by leaving behind a speck of blood, dropping a sweat-stained hat, or even taking a sip from a can of soda, they can give the police everything they need to identify and arrest them.

In the first decade of the twenty-first century the main tools used by the police include

- questioning witnesses and suspects
- searching the crime scene for physical evidence
- employing informants and undercover agents
- investigating the whereabouts of previous offenders when a crime they've been known to commit has occurred
- using computer databases to match evidence found on one crime scene to that found on others or to previously arrested suspects
- sharing information with other law enforcement agencies via the Internet
- using modern communications to keep the public informed and enlist their aid in ongoing investigations

But just as they have many different tools with which to solve crime, so too do they have many different kinds of crime and criminals to investigate. There is murder, kidnapping, and bank robbery. There are financial crimes committed by con men who gain their victim's trust or computer experts who hack into computers. There are criminals who have formed themselves into gangs and those who are organized into national syndicates. And there are those who would kill as many people as possible, either for the thrill of taking a human life or in the horribly misguided belief that it will advance their cause.

The Criminal Investigations series looks at all of the above and more. Each book in the series takes one type of crime and gives the reader an overview of the history of the crime, the methods and motives behind it, the people who have committed it, and the means by which these people are caught and punished. In this series celebrity crimes will be discussed and exposed. Mysteries that have yet to be solved will be presented. Readers will discover the truth about murderers, serial killers, and bank robbers whose stories have become myths and legends. These books will explain how criminals can separate a person from his hard-earned cash, how they prey on the weak and helpless, what is being done to stop them, and what one can do to help prevent becoming a victim.

John L. French,
Crime Scene Supervisor,
Baltimore Police Crime Laboratory

* Federal Bureau of Investigation. "Uniform Crime Reports, Crime in the United States 2000." Available online. URL: http://www.fbi.gov/ucr/00cius.htm. Accessed January 11, 2008.

Introduction

Americans adore celebrities. From the earliest days of Hollywood filmmaking to the tabloid frenzy over photographs of Angelina Jolie's first baby in 2006, the public's fascination with "superstars" has fueled a multibillion-dollar *infotainment* industry where news and publicity stunts collide, blurring the lines between truth and fantasy.

But the obsession with celebrity, while trivial, may also have a darker side. As much as fans love watching singers, actors, athletes, or high-fashion models on the rise, they also love to watch them fall. Divorce, disgrace, and death all feed the media machine.

Throughout history, society has nurtured heroes. Royalty and warriors were the earliest celebrities. Victory in battle might bring fame and fortune, but the fickle public's mood could change with deadly consequences, as in Julius Caesar's case. Other early celebrities, like Rome's Caligula, destroyed themselves through madness and excess.

It is a pattern repeated all too often in the present day.

In the early twentieth century, athletes and explorers joined war heroes on the short list of celebrities. Achievement was still the key to fame in those days: Babe Ruth's home-run record in baseball; Jack Dempsey's run of knockouts in the boxing ring; Charles Lindbergh's solo flight across the Atlantic Ocean. Celebrities still had to *do something*, but their deeds no longer affected the fate of nations.

By the 1920s and early 1930s, America's first movie stars had staked their claim to flamboyant headlines, rating coverage for both their films and their off-camera scandals. At the same time, Prohibition and the Great Depression spawned a new breed of celebrity outlaws such as Al Capone, Dutch Schultz, and "Baby

Face" Nelson, whose violent crimes provided a modern equivalent to ancient Rome's bloody games in the Coliseum.

Today, while most celebrities become famous through some achievement—acting, singing, an athletic skill—a new class has arisen, idolized simply for their appearance (as with supermodels) or their wealth. Sisters Paris and Nicky Hilton, heirs to the fortune of hotel magnate Conrad Hilton (1887–1979), offer a case in point, as both were famous for years as "party girls" before they tried their hands at film, music, or modeling.

The failures of celebrities excite Americans as much as any of their notable successes. The most thrilling tales are found where fame and crime collide.

As much as fans love to watch celebrities excel, they enjoy with equal zeal watching the famous lose their fortunes, go to jail, or even die. It does not seem to matter if celebrities are criminals or victims.

Either way, their pain and suffering is news.

Celebrities and Crime examines that phenomenon, while following the methods used by police and forensic scientists to investigate crimes involving celebrities. Each chapter surveys a specific famous case, revealing how celebrity itself affects the justice system for better or worse.

Chapters 1 through 9 are chronologically arranged, reviewing some notorious cases from the early 1930s through 2005.

Chapter 1, "Kidnapped!," examines the still-controversial Lindbergh kidnapping to determine if justice was served, and how the victim's fame affected the outcome.

Chapter 2, "The Devil's Business," recounts the infamous Manson Family murders of 1969, which targeted actress Sharon Tate and other wealthy victims in Los Angeles.

Chapter 3, "Tarnished Hero," reviews the still-unsolved murder of actor Bob Crane, star of the TV comedy series *Hogan's Heroes.*

Chapter 4, "Stalked!," spotlights the phenomenon of celebrity stalkers, including the slayer of ex-Beatle John Lennon and would-be presidential assassin John Hinckley.

In Chapter 5, "Let Us Prey," we penetrate the world of millionaire televangelists to review the crimes of Jim and Tammy Bakker.

Chapter 6, "Murder in Brentwood," examines the O.J. Simpson murder case and the very different verdicts obtained in two separate trials.

Chapter 7, "Number One with a Bullet," details the "East-West feud" between rival rap stars Tupac Shakur and Notorious B.I.G., which resulted in the death of both artists.

Chapter 8, "Sticky Fingers," investigates the quality of celebrity justice, highlighted by the shoplifting trial of actress Winona Ryder.

Chapter 9, "A Shot in the Dark," examines the mysterious murder of the wife of actor Robert Blake—and the highly controversial trials that followed.

Finally, Chapter 10, "The Price of Fame," examines why and how celebrities are treated differently by the police and courts, in a society where all persons are said—at least on paper—to be equal.

Kidnapped!

The world's most famous baby had been sleeping peacefully since 8 p.m. on March 1, 1932. His live-in nanny checked each hour to make sure his rest was undisturbed. At 9 p.m. she found him safely tucked in bed. When she checked again at 10 p.m., his crib was empty.

She told the boy's mother, who suggested that his father—a well-known prankster—might have taken little Charlie as a joke. Instead of laughing, Charlie's father rushed upstairs to check the nursery and then grabbed a rifle and began to search the house and grounds. He found a ransom note in Charlie's room, and a ladder propped against the wall outside.

Police were summoned at 10:25 p.m.

It was too late.

THE LONE EAGLE

Charles A. Lindbergh Jr. (1902–74), the son of a U.S. Congressman and a chemistry teacher, was born in Detroit, Michigan. His interest in flight and mechanics drew him into the U.S. Army Air Service, and later to worldwide fame. In the 1920s, while flying as a pilot for one of America's first airmail routes, Lindbergh decided to attempt a feat that would put his name in the history books: a solo flight across the Atlantic Ocean.

At least 80 other pilots had crossed the Atlantic since 1919, but Lindbergh was the first to make it alone, in a 34-hour nonstop flight on May 20–21, 1927. On arrival in Paris, Lindbergh received the French Legion of Honor, but that was only the first of his honors.

When Lindbergh returned to the United States, a fleet of navy warships escorted him to Washington, D.C., where President Calvin Coolidge gave Lindbergh a Distinguished Flying Cross. Lindbergh also collected a $25,000 reward (worth $250,000 today), which was offered in 1919 for the first solo trans-Atlantic pilot. On June 13 a massive parade was held to celebrate Lindbergh's visit to New York City. Two years later, he received the Congressional Medal of Honor for heroism.

Fame and fortune followed Lindbergh—dubbed the "Lone Eagle" by reporters—yet he seemed to find his greatest happiness at home. Lindbergh married Ann Morrow, the only woman he ever dated, and their first son was born in 1930. Newspapers called Charles III "the Eaglet." To escape the press, Lindbergh bought a 390-acre estate north of Hopewell, New Jersey, where his family lived happily until the night of March 1, 1932.

HELD FOR RANSOM

The ransom note found on the nursery windowsill was riddled with spelling errors, but its meaning was clear. The kidnapper demanded $50,000 in cash and warned Lindbergh not to call the police.

In fact, dozens of state and local officers were on the scene within an hour, trampling over evidence—including two reported sets of footprints near the ladder found outside—that could have helped identify the kidnapper. By the time a fingerprint expert arrived, at midnight, no useful prints remained on the ransom note. As for the homemade ladder with its top wrung broken, officers were stumped.

New Jersey State Police, led by Colonel Herbert Schwarzkopf— father of Gulf War commander "Stormin' Norman" Schwarzkopf— soon took charge of the investigation. While the Federal Bureau of Investigation had no jurisdiction in kidnapping cases, President Herbert Hoover vowed that he would "move Heaven and Earth" to recover the Lindbergh baby. Soon, the new Lindbergh Law would make interstate kidnapping a federal offense, but it came too late for the Eaglet.

While a $75,000 reward for the child's safe return brought many false leads, the Lindberghs received three more ransom demands, postmarked from Brooklyn, New York. One letter fell into a journalist's hands, and copies were sold on street corners for $5 each. The last angry letter doubled the ransom demand to $100,000.

Police investigators reconstruct details of the kidnapping at the Lindbergh estate in Hopewell, N.J., in December 1934. The ladder shown in the picture is suspected to be the one used in the kidnapping of the 19-month-old son of world-famous aviator Charles Lindbergh. *AP*

"JAFSIE" AND "CEMETERY JOHN"

Enter John F. Condon, an elderly eccentric from the Bronx, often known from his initials (J.F.C.) as "Jafsie." After writing a letter to the press, offering $1,000 of his own money for the Lindbergh child, Condon received an alleged note from the kidnappers. Based on that note alone, the Lindberghs accepted Jafsie as their go-between with the abductors.

After tense negotiations, Condon met a man who called himself John, at New York's Woodlawn Cemetery. Condon never saw the stranger's face, but said he "sounded foreign." John described himself as part of a five-person gang, which had young Charlie hidden on a boat. Condon demanded proof, and John promised to send the baby's sleeping suit. He also agreed to a ransom of $70,000.

A few days later, Condon received a toddler's sleeping suit by mail. Although it was a common style, with no specific markings, Lindbergh identified the suit as his son's. Condon then arranged to deliver the ransom on April 2.

That night, Condon and Lindbergh took the money to St. Raymond's Cemetery in the Bronx. Agent Elmer Irey of the Internal Revenue Service had recommended payment in obsolete gold certificates, with their serial numbers recorded.

♀ A QUESTION OF IDENTITY

Researchers still debate the fate of Charles Lindbergh III. The corpse found in April 1932 lacked one leg and both hands. Its skull was crushed, and the rest was badly decomposed. Lindbergh and Betty Gow identified the body from a shirt and a slight deformity of the right foot, while the baby's doctor refused to confirm if the child was a boy or a girl.

Detective Ellis Parker—nicknamed "America's Sherlock Holmes" —noted that the corpse was 33 inches long, while Charles III measured only 29 inches two weeks before the kidnapping. Parker also thought the corpse was too decomposed for a body dead only one month. He suggested that local bootleggers, disturbed by intense police activity around Hopewell, had provided a corpse to "close" the case. Since DNA testing was unknown until the 1980s, we have no final proof of the dead child's identity. Because the corpse was cremated after being identified, it is not available for DNA testing today.

Over the years, several men came forward claiming to be the lost Lindbergh child and seeking a share of the family's estate. The last, in October 2000, was proved a fraud by DNA testing, but some researchers still believe the Lindbergh baby lived with a new family after the kidnapping.

At the drop, while Lindbergh watched from a distance, Condon gave $50,000 to "Cemetery John," as he'd been dubbed, claiming he could raise no more. Without showing his face, John took the cash and left a note directing searchers to a boat moored at Martha's Vineyard, Massachusetts. Officers soon learned that no such boat existed. Lindbergh admitted that he had been tricked.

Six weeks later, on May 12, a trucker found part of a toddler's corpse in the New Jersey woods, less than five miles from the Lindbergh home. Police had searched the area in March and found nothing. Lindbergh and nanny Betty Gow identified the corpse, but Charlie's doctor refused, saying that he could not identify the body "for $10 million." In fact, he could not even say if the corpse was male or female.[1]

Despite that confusion, police launched a murder investigation, assisted by federal agents. Suspecting an "inside job," detectives questioned the Lindberghs' maid, Violet Sharpe. She lied about her whereabouts on March 1, and later committed suicide to avoid re-questioning.

TRACING THE RANSOM

Agent Irey's plan paid off when gold certificates from the Lindbergh ransom began to surface. Unfortunately, they appeared in various locations from New York to Minneapolis and Chicago. A German immigrant named Gerhardt spent $2,980 of the ransom in New York in May 1932. Police traced Gerhardt much later, and his son-in-law committed suicide after interrogation, but no charges were filed.

By then, the case had been "solved."

In September 1934 police jailed another German immigrant, Bruno Hauptmann (1899–1936), one day after he passed a ransom bill at a Bronx gas station. Hauptmann had entered the United States illegally in 1923, then married and worked as a carpenter.

Police found $14,000 of the Lindbergh ransom money in Hauptmann's garage and later claimed that a board from his attic floor was used as part of the crude kidnap ladder. They also found Condon's phone number written inside Hauptmann's closet. Some handwriting experts claimed that Hauptmann wrote the ransom notes, while others disagreed.

Three facsimiles of handwriting used as evidence against Bruno Hauptmann. *Top:* Hauptmann's signature on an auto registration card. *Middle:* Hauptmann's signature reconstructed from letters cut out of the ransom note. *Bottom:* The final ransom note sent to the Lindberghs. *Bettmann/Corbis*

Hauptmann refused to confess, despite a doctor's testimony that he was badly beaten in jail. He pled not guilty to murder and kidnapping charges.

A MEDIA CIRCUS

Journalist H.L. Mencken called Hauptmann's trial "the biggest story since the Resurrection." Reporters from around the world flocked to Flemington, New Jersey, for the great event. Newsman Tom Cassidy admitted writing Jafsie's phone number in Hauptmann's closet, but authorities still used it as "evidence" against Hauptmann.

Worse yet were the prosecution's supposed eyewitnesses. Two Hopewell locals, who had denied seeing any suspicious prowlers in March 1932, changed their stories and "identified" Hauptmann at trial, after receiving cash rewards. Jafsie identified Hauptmann as Cemetery John only after police threatened him with arrest as an accomplice to murder. Charles Lindbergh likewise said he was unable to identify "John" in 1932, but later picked Hauptmann by his voice alone.

Hauptmann denied any part in the crime. He claimed that the money found at his home came from Isidor Fisch, a fellow immigrant who had returned to Germany and died there in 1934. Prosecutors belittled the "Fisch story," and jurors convicted Hauptmann on February 13, 1935. He received a death sentence.

In prison, while awaiting execution, Hauptmann still proclaimed his innocence. He rejected a newspaper's $90,000 offer for a full confession, and later refused Governor Harold Hoffman's last-minute offer of a life prison term in exchange for admission of guilt. Hauptmann died in the electric chair on April 3, 1936.

AFTERMATH

Although the Lindberghs had five more children between 1932 and 1945, they never recovered from the loss of young Charlie. In December 1935 they moved to Europe, seeking greater privacy.

There, Charles Lindbergh traveled widely and became friendly with Herman Göring, commander of Nazi Germany's air force. In 1938 Göring gave Lindbergh Germany's Medal of Honor for his flight in 1927. American diplomats protested, but Lindbergh kept the medal and praised Germany's superior military forces. As a spokesman for the isolationist America First Committee, he blamed Jews for advocating war against Germany, and offered to negotiate a peace treaty with Nazi leader Adolf Hitler.

Lindbergh's support for Germany damaged his reputation, particularly after America entered World War II in December 1941. Semi-retired from public life, Lindbergh published a memoir of his 1927 flight in 1953, which won the Pulitzer Prize. He died on August 26, 1974. Ann Lindbergh died on February 7, 2001.

ENDURING CONTROVERSY

Seven decades after the Lindbergh kidnapping, controversy still surrounds the case. Published theories include

- a ransom kidnapping by organized gangsters from Chicago or Detroit
- conspiracy between the Lindberghs' maid, Violet Sharpe, and unidentified accomplices
- kidnapping by the Gerhardt family
- kidnapping by Isidor Fisch, a convicted swindler in his native Germany
- deliberate murder by Ann Lindbergh's jealous sister, disguised as kidnapping to spare the family from scandal
- accidental death, caused by Ann dropping Charlie, concealed as a crime to avoid embarrassment

More than a dozen books and countless articles have debated the Lindbergh kidnapping case. Novelist Max Alan Collins offered a clever fictional solution in *Stolen Away* (1991), while two movies have dramatized the events. Anthony Hopkins—later Hollywood's Dr. Hannibal Lecter—played Hauptmann in *The Lindbergh Kidnapping Case* (1976). Stephen Rea portrayed an innocent Hauptmann in HBO's *Crime of the Century* (1996).

The Devil's Business

Terror gripped the city of Los Angeles in the summer of 1969. On two successive August nights, unknown prowlers brutally killed seven victims in their homes, mutilating the bodies and writing slogans on the walls in blood. The first attack claimed five lives, including actress Sharon Tate and millionaire coffee heiress Abigail Folger. As summer turned to fall, no suspects were identified, and authorities could suggest no motive for the vicious crimes.

A RISING STAR

Sharon Tate (1943–69) was born in Texas and traveled widely as a child with her military family. Renowned from infancy for her striking good looks, she was named "Miss Tiny Tot of Dallas" as a baby, and later won "Miss Richland, Washington," at age 16. She began modeling a year later, while living with her parents in Verona, Italy.

When a Hollywood film crew came to town, Tate won her first role as an extra in *Hemingway's Adventures of a Young Man* (1962). A second uncredited part in *Barabbas* (1962) prompted Tate to leave Italy for Hollywood, where she appeared on television's *Mr. Ed* and *The Beverly Hillbillies.* Her movie roles included *The Americanization of Emily* (1964) and *Eye of the Devil* (1967).

Eye of the Devil was filmed in France, where Tate met 34-year-old director Roman Polanski, a son of Polish immigrants whose family suffered Nazi persecution during the Holocaust. Polanski cast Tate as the female lead in his new film, *The Fearless Vampire Killers* (1967), and they soon fell in love. When Tate returned to the United States to star in *Don't Make Waves* (1967), Polanski followed her.

Meanwhile, Tate's film career was blossoming. Her fourth movie of 1967, *Valley of the Dolls,* received national publicity (much of it negative). Men's magazines, including *Esquire* and *Playboy,* promoted Tate as a symbol of the "Swinging Sixties." *Newsweek*'s reviewer hated *Valley of the Dolls* but called Tate "one of the most smashing young things to hit Hollywood in a long time."

Tate married Polanski in January 1968, and they bought a home on Cielo Drive in Los Angeles. The couple entertained frequently, and their social set included rock stars, Hollywood's leading performers, and Polanski's friends from Europe. In December 1968, Tate announced that her first child would be born in late August 1969.

Meanwhile, she made more films, appearing in *Rosemary's Baby* (1968), *The Wrecking Crew* (1969), and *12 + 1* (also called *The 13 Chairs;* 1969). She received a Golden Globe nomination as "New Star of the Year," and the *Motion Picture Herald* named Tate a runner-up for "The Star of Tomorrow." The future looked bright, with more movie offers and better reviews for Tate's new comic roles.

HELTER SKELTER

Tate entertained friends on the night of August 8, 1969, two weeks before her child was due. Polanski was in London at the time. Tate's guests included Abigail Folger, Folger's boyfriend Wojciech Frykowski, and Hollywood hairdresser Jay Sebring. Steven Parent, a young friend of Tate's caretaker, was also present when prowlers arrived, sometime after 11:30 p.m.

The intruders shot Parent in his car, in Tate's driveway, then crept into the house. As later described by one who was present, the gang's leader told Tate and her friends, "I'm here to do the Devil's business." Folger and Frykowski fled, but both were stabbed to death on the front lawn. Inside, the gang bound Tate and Sebring, and then stabbed them both repeatedly. Tate suffered 16 knife wounds. The killers wrote "PIG" on the wall in Tate's blood.

While police grilled Tate's caretaker and Polanski flew home from Europe, the killers struck again on August 9. Los Angeles residents Leno and Rosemary LaBianca died at their home, stabbed with knives and a barbecue fork. The slayers left more bloody graffiti: "WAR," "DEATH TO PIGS," and "HEALTER SKELTER."

Aerial view of the home of Sharon Tate and Roman Polanski, where Mrs. Tate and four other people were found murdered on August 9, 1969. One body is under the sheet in front of the house at the upper left. Another is in the automobile at the lower right. Another was found near the swimming pool at the top and two others were found in the house. *AP*

Police felt the media's pressure to solve the murders. *Life* magazine ran photos of the crime scenes, while newspaper headlines and TV reports spoke of ritual slayings. L.A.'s police were desperate.

But where were the killers?

BREAKING THE CASE

Despite the evidence recovered from both crimes, police still had no suspects until November, when they got a lucky break. A car-theft suspect, Susan Atkins, bragged to cellmates that she had participated in the murders. Soon, investigators traced her movements to the Spahn Ranch in Death Valley, often used in Western films. There, officers arrested several members of a strange communal group known as the "Family."

Its leader, Charles Manson, was a 35-year-old drifter who had spent most of his life behind bars on various charges. Paroled over his own objections in March 1967, he had spent the intervening years immersed in California's "hippie" subculture, collecting younger runaways and petty criminals as members of his "family." They wandered aimlessly, stole cars, ate out of garbage cans, and begged for cash. Drugs and bizarre religious practices became the focus of their lives.

Based on statements from Atkins and other Family members, police charged Manson, Atkins, and five others with nine counts of murder. Aside from the seven Tate-LaBianca killings, charges were also filed in the deaths of musician Gary Hinman (July 1969) and movie stuntman Donald Shea (August 1969). Linda Kasabian agreed to testify against her fellow defendants, in return for immunity.

According to Kasabian and others, Manson was obsessed with the music of the Beatles, a British rock group whose songs allegedly contained predictions of a coming race war in America. Manson called the war "Helter Skelter," the title of one Beatles song (misspelled by the LaBianca killers), predicting that its survivors would come to Death Valley in search of his leadership.

Beyond that fantasy, Manson hoped to launch Helter Skelter by blaming African Americans for murders of wealthy white victims. He sent his "children" out to kill and ordered them to mark their crime scenes with phrases familiar from the speeches of black militants.

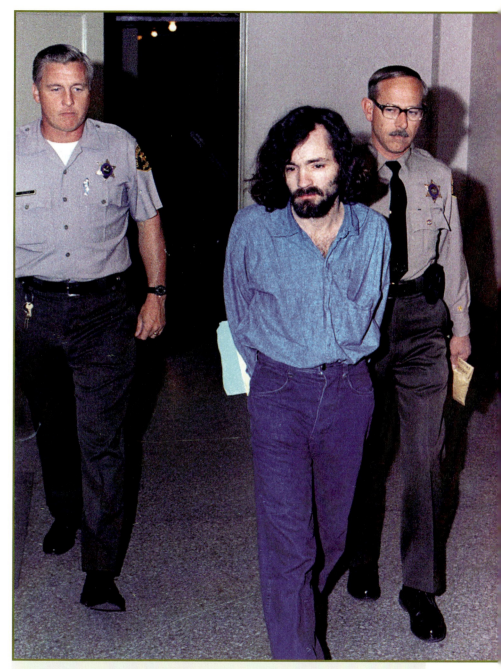

Deputy sheriffs escort Charles Manson on his way to court in Los Angeles in August 1970. *AP*

Jurors convicted Manson, Atkins, Patricia Krenwinkel, and Leslie Van Houten of the Tate-LaBianca murders in March 1971. All four were sentenced to death. A second jury convicted and condemned Charles "Tex" Watson for the same crimes in October 1971. In other trials, Manson and two more family members, Robert Beausoleil and Steven Grogan, were sentenced to die for the Hinman-Shea killings. Before any were executed, however, the U.S. Supreme Court overturned all current death sentences in 1972, commuting the verdicts to life imprisonment.

Manson and his "children" are now eligible for parole, but only one has been released from prison. Authorities freed Steven Grogan on November 18, 1985.

♀ CRUEL AND UNUSUAL?

More than 35 years after the Manson death penalties were overturned, fierce controversy still surrounds American capital punishment. All member nations of the European Union have abandoned executions, but recent polls in the United States show that 69 percent of Americans support capital punishment—this, despite the fact that 53 percent believe executions have little or no effect in deterring violent crimes.

According to official records as researched and tallied by M. Watt Espy and John Ortiz Smykla, 14,175 persons were executed for various crimes in Colonial America and the United States between 1608 and 1972.[1] In the latter year, the Supreme Court ruled that all existing capital punishment statutes violated the U.S. Constitution's Eighth Amendment ban on "cruel and unusual punishment." Later rulings permitted executions under stricter, more uniform guidelines. New laws were passed, and executions resumed in January 1977, with 1,024 inmates killed through May 2006.[2]

Critics of capital punishment note that 67 percent of all American death-penalty verdicts are overturned on appeal, while DNA testing has freed more than 100 wrongfully convicted inmates since the early 1990s. Supporters use various moral, religious, and economic arguments in favor of executions. Thirty-six of the 50 states presently endorse capital punishment, but three of those have performed no executions since 1972.

Former L.A. prosecutor Vincent Bugliosi suggests, in his book *Helter Skelter* (1974), that the Family killed at least 36 victims, including one in England and Manson's biological father in Kentucky. No further charges were filed in the remaining 27 cases.

AFTERMATH

Roman Polanski continued his career as a film director after wife Sharon's murder, drawing criticism in some cases for his graphic depiction of violence in movies such as *Chinatown* (1974) and *The Tenant* (1976).

Ten years after the Manson trial, when Leslie Van Houten gathered 900 signatures on a petition supporting her parole, Doris Tate (Sharon's mother) fought back with a petition bearing 350,000 names, to keep Van Houten in prison. Over the next 10 years, until her death in July 1992, Tate attended every parole hearing for her daughter's killers and argued successfully against their release. Thanks to Tate, in 1982 California passed laws permitting crime victims or their survivors to speak at hearings where convicted felons are sentenced or considered for parole. Sharon Tate's sister Patti continued her mother's work from 1992 to 2000, founding the Doris Tate Crime Victims Bureau to promote similar laws throughout America. Debra Tate, Sharon's last remaining sister, has since taken up the cause.

While Charles Manson makes a joke of his periodic parole hearings, other members of the Family still seek release on a regular basis. Charles Watson has become a minister in prison, with a wife and children outside who collect donations for his "church." Susan Atkins briefly married a preacher and published an autobiography, *Child of Satan, Child of God* (1978), describing her religious conversion. Leslie Van Houten argues for parole on grounds that she regrets her crimes and has matured in prison.

The reverse side of that coin is seen in other Family members. On September 5, 1975, Lynette "Squeaky" Fromme tried to shoot President Gerald Ford in Sacramento, California, but her pistol misfired. She later received a life prison term and remains in custody today. Three months after the bungled shooting, Sandra Good—Fromme's roommate and another Family member—was arrested for sending threats through the U.S. mail. She received a 10-year sentence and was freed in 1985.

The Manson Family exerts ongoing fascination for the American public. Aside from numerous nonfiction books on the group and its crimes, Bugliosi's *Helter Skelter* has been filmed twice as a made-for-TV movie—in 1976, with actor Steve Railsback portraying Manson, and again in 2004, with Jeffrey Davies in the starring role. Michael Perry's fictional novel *Skelter* (1994) describes a plot by Manson's son to break him out of prison—a scheme that *almost* succeeds.

Tarnished Hero

Shortly after 2 p.m. on June 29, 1978, Victoria Berry called at the Scottsdale, Arizona, home of fellow actor Bob Crane. They had been scheduled for a luncheon interview at noon, but Crane never showed. Berry was concerned since he had not called to cancel.

No one answered Berry's knock, so she tried the front door and found it unlocked. Calling out Crane's name, she entered a living room littered with clothing, magazines, and video equipment.

Berry crossed the room, peered through a window at the backyard swimming pool, and saw no one there. Still calling out to Crane, she moved on to the bedroom, where a figure lay huddled in Crane's bed.

At first, she thought it was a girl with long red hair. Then Berry realized that she was seeing blood, lots of it, soaking through Crane's sheets and pillow, even spattered on the wall.

She ran to telephone police.

DRUMMING UP SUCCESS

Robert Edward Crane (1928–78) was a Connecticut native who dropped out of high school to play drums with a dance band. That musical connection led him into radio and television broadcasting, but fame remained elusive. His first TV job was at a station that seemed to have no audience. When Crane offered $100 to the first viewer who called in, no one claimed the free money.

Crane moved his family to Hollywood in 1956, pursuing his career as a disc jockey. His new show was a hit, with celebrity guests including Frank Sinatra, Marilyn Monroe, Bob Hope, and Marvin Gaye. Soon, Crane earned a reputation as "King of the L.A.

Airwaves," earning more than $100,000 per year, but he craved something more.

In 1961, at age 33, Crane turned to acting. Before year's end, he landed roles in two films, *Man-Trap* and *Return to Peyton Place*. His next big break, in 1963, was a regular part on TV's popular *Donna Reed Show*, but producers wrote him out of the show in 1965, saying his performance as a playboy neighbor of the series stars was "too suggestive" for a family program.

Naturally, Crane was disappointed by that setback, but success was just around the corner. He would find it when he took the biggest gamble of his career.

A RISKY HIT

Twenty years had passed since the end of World War II, but memories of that devastating conflict still haunted many of its participants, from combat veterans to survivors of the Nazi Holocaust. It seemed bizarre, therefore, when writers Bernard Fein and Albert Ruddy proposed a TV situation comedy involving Allied soldiers in a German prison camp, similar to the 1953 film *Stalag 17*.

Somehow, the series was approved at CBS—ironically, with Jewish actors Werner Klemperer and John Banner cast as the camp's bumbling Nazis in charge, Col. Wilhelm Klink and Sgt. Hans Schultz. Bob Crane won the lead role as wisecracking Col. Robert E. Hogan, who always managed to outwit the foes with a smile.

Against all expectations, *Hogan's Heroes* was an instant hit. Crane received two Emmy nominations (1966 and 1967), but failed to take home the awards. Werner Klemperer won Emmys for his performances in 1967 and 1968. Crane's love affair with actress Patti Olsen (cast as Klink's secretary) led him to divorce, and he married Olsen on the *Hogan's Heroes* set in October 1970.

Later that year, network executives decided to shift their audience focus, seeking younger and wealthier viewers. Despite its continued high ratings, *Hogan's Heroes* was canceled in 1971, along with several other popular shows. Crane and his cast mates were stunned.

Worse yet, despite six years of critical success, Crane received few offers for new film or TV projects. Over the next five years, he appeared in two movies for children, *Superdad* (1973) and *Gus*

Bob Crane in costume in a publicity photo for *Hogan's Heroes*.
Bettmann/Corbis

(1976). NBC executives bought the *Bob Crane Show* in 1975, but ratings lagged, and it got the axe after only three months on-air.

That failure deepened Crane's depression and brought to the forefront a side of his character rarely glimpsed by fans.

THE DARK SIDE

Since his teens, Bob Crane had been obsessed with sex. He talked about it constantly to friends, collected mountains of pornography, and barely masked his tendencies in public with off-color jokes and aggressive flirting. Crane's constant infidelity and his obsession with pornographic videotapes—often starring himself with multiple women—doomed his second marriage. Wife Patti filed for divorce in 1977.

Finally, even on camera—as when he taped an episode of *Celebrity Cooks*, in January 1978—Crane could not resist dropping inappropriate sexual jokes into every conversation. That show never aired. By the time it was scheduled for broadcast, on July 10, 1978, Bob Crane was dead, murdered in his own home.

Crane's porn addiction led him to Scottsdale resident John Carpenter (1928–98), a part-time actor and electronics expert who specialized in video recordings. Carpenter enjoyed socializing with celebrities, taping their frolics, and—at least in Crane's case—sharing their girlfriends.

On June 28, 1978, Crane and Carpenter had breakfast together, then went shopping in Scottsdale for video equipment. Put off by high prices, Crane borrowed a new recorder from one of his friends, and then visited a girlfriend's home for several hours. That night, he went barhopping with Carpenter, but they failed to meet any willing women. According to Carpenter, they split up and Crane went home around 2:30 a.m. on June 29.

MURDER

Crane's last hours are shrouded in mystery. Police, summoned by Victoria Berry, found him beaten to death in bed, with a cord from a video recorder tied around his neck. A bottle of Scotch whisky stood on the nightstand, but Berry told detectives Crane never drank

♀ REAL-LIFE CSI: BLOODSTAIN EVIDENCE

Bloodstain pattern evidence may be vital to the reconstruction of a crime. Using mathematics and physics, forensic scientists can calculate the force delivered by a blow in feet-per-second or the movements of the people involved, based on the shape and direction of blood drops, smears, swipes, wipes, or other stains found on floors, walls, ceilings, furniture, and so on. Such evidence may also help investigators track the motions of a victim and attacker at a crime scene, even when no victim is present and the offender is unknown. It is most useful in cases involving more than one killer or victim.

Types of blood-spatter evidence include:

Arterial spurting, distinctive wavelike spurts of blood produced from severed arteries while the victim's heart is still beating.

Cast-off patterns, created when some bloody object (a fist, club, etc.) is swung with enough force to spray drops of blood onto surrounding surfaces.

Back spatter, caused by the impact of a weapon or bullet that makes blood from a fresh wound spurt back toward the weapon, rather than in the direction of impact, or when blood sprays from an axe or club as the wielder pulls it back for another blow. In close-range gunshots, blood may stain the shooter's hands or weapon, even the inside of a gun barrel, which is one reason guns found at crime scenes should not be picked up by sticking a pen or pencil into the barrel.

Forward spatter, traveling in the direction of impact from a weapon or projectile, as when blood sprays from a gunshot exit wound.

Drip patterns, created when blood drops fall from any height onto a lower surface, such as pavement or a floor. *Parent drops* are the large, roughly circular drops found in drip patterns, surrounded by smaller cast-off droplets called *satellites.* The bigger the drop, the higher the height from which it fell.

Scotch. No evidence suggested a break-in, causing police to suspect that Crane invited his killer into the house.

But who was it?

Patti Crane sometimes fought violently with her soon-to-be ex-husband, but she was in Washington State when he died. From the extent of Crane's injuries and bloodstain evidence found at the scene, Medical Examiner Heinz Karnitschnig profiled the unknown killer as a "very strong man."

Unfortunately, Crane's promiscuous lifestyle offered countless suspects in the persons of jealous husbands and lovers. One man, whose girlfriend Crane filmed, had taped a mutilated photo of Crane on the actor's door. The severed video cord around Crane's neck also suggested a connection to his porn hobby.

Or did it?

Some investigators thought the cord represented a severed *friendship,* casting suspicion on John Carpenter. Acquaintances claimed that Carpenter wanted a closer relationship with Crane than Crane would tolerate. Some suggested that Carpenter was gay, and that he may have made advances that disturbed Crane. Was rejection, then, the motive for Crane's slaying?

On June 29, three hours before Victoria Berry found Crane's body, Carpenter flew to Los Angeles. At 3:10 p.m., he telephoned Crane's home and police answered the call. Carpenter identified himself and answered certain questions, but he never asked why officers were at Crane's home.

Scottsdale police later examined Carpenter's rented car and found small human bloodstains. The blood was Type B, shared by Crane and 10 percent of America's population at large. Carpenter denied any part in Crane's murder and could not explain the bloodstains in his car.

DNA testing procedures for blood did not exist in 1978. British scientists developed the test in 1985, but when Arizona investigators tested the stains from Carpenter's car in 1989, seeking a match to Bob Crane, the results were inconclusive.

ALMOST SOLVED

It was no secret that police suspected Carpenter of killing Crane. Wherever Carpenter went, the unspoken accusation followed him. In June 1992, when police finally charged him with Crane's murder, Carpenter expressed relief that he would have a chance to clear his name in court.

John Carpenter talks with his attorney in a Los Angeles courtroom in June 1992. He was charged with the 1978 murder of actor and friend Bob Crane. Carpenter was acquitted by a jury in 1994.
Douglas C. Pizac/AP

After 14 years of delay, police based their murder charge on a photograph of Carpenter's rental car from 1978. The photo showed a tiny speck of *something*, barely 1/16 inch in diameter, stuck to one of the auto's door panels. The evidence itself was long gone, but criminalists claimed they could identify it from the photo as human brain tissue, even though such identification based on a photograph alone is impossible.

At trial, in 1994, prosecution witnesses offered that photo to the jury. Defense experts testified that the "speck" could not be identified as *anything* without proper laboratory tests. Prosecutors fired back with a 16-year-old videotape of Carpenter, Crane, and an unnamed woman in bed. They claimed that Crane had threatened to break off his friendship with Carpenter, thus ending Carpenter's access to beautiful women, which drove Carpenter into a murderous rage.

In fact, however, the state offered no evidence that Crane had ended his friendship with Carpenter. Their outing on June 28, 1978, appeared to prove the opposite. Jurors acquitted Carpenter of all charges. He died four years later, from a heart attack.

In 2002 director Paul Schrader released the film *Auto Focus* about Crane's life and murder. Crane's son Scott denounced the film's portrayal of his father.

Stalked!

At 10:50 p.m. on December 8, 1980, world-famous musician John Lennon and his wife, Yoko Ono, returned home from a recording session. As they approached the entrance to their apartment building, The Dakota (near Manhattan's Central Park), a man stepped from the shadows and called out, "Mr. Lennon!" As Lennon turned, the stranger raised a pistol and shot him five times, inflicting fatal wounds. The gunman then sat down on the curb nearby to wait for police.

Officers identified the killer as 25-year-old Mark David Chapman, a former drug addict and mental patient who claimed a long-time fascination with Lennon (though he never spoke of it to family or friends). Chapman had approached Lennon at 4 p.m. the same day and obtained Lennon's autograph outside The Dakota.

Chapman told police that he shot Lennon in order to "make a statement." Some conspiracy theorists believe he was a hired assassin. At trial, Chapman's lawyers recommended an insanity plea, but Chapman insisted that "the little voices inside my head told me to plead guilty." He received a prison term of 20 years to life.

STALKERS AT LARGE

While Mark Chapman's crime brought to light the dangers of obsessive fans, he was not the first celebrity stalker on record—or the last. Instances of celebrity stalking can sometimes last for years. Some famous celebrity stalking cases are described in the following chronology:

Legendary musician John Lennon was murdered outside his Manhattan apartment building on December 8, 1980. *Penny Tweedie/Corbis*

1949: Ruth Ann Steinhagen wounded pro baseball player Eddie Waitkus with a rifle shot. Police found photos of Waitkus at the teenager's home. She was sent to a mental institution and released three years later.

1969: Chester Young, obsessed with singer Peggy Lennon of the Lennon Sisters (no relation to John Lennon), shot and killed Peggy's father. Two months later, Young committed suicide with the same pistol.

1981: Seeking to impress actress Jodie Foster, with whom he was obsessed, John Hinckley Jr. attempted to kill President Ronald Reagan in March. He wounded Reagan and three others with pistol fire in Washington, D.C. Acquitted on grounds of insanity, he remains confined to a psychiatric hospital (where he once corresponded with Charles Manson).

1982: Arthur Richard Jackson stabbed actress Theresa Saldana in March, acting on "orders from God." Saldana survived her wounds. Jackson served 14 years and was then extradited to England on robbery charges.

1983: Michael Perry regarded singer Olivia Newton-John as "a muse who was granted everlasting life." Security officers caught Perry on Newton-John's property in 1983 and sent him home to Louisiana—where he killed his parents and three other relatives. Perry received a death sentence for his crimes.

1984: Ralph Nau also stalked Olivia Newton-John from 1980 to 1984, when he leaped on stage with her at a concert in Australia. Deported back to Illinois, Nau murdered his brother and was then declared insane.

1984–1999: Edwin John Carlson stalked country singer Barbara Mandrell and her family for 15 years, beginning in 1984. He was finally jailed for invading Mandrell's home, but she declined to press charges. Back in his native Minnesota, Carlson faced criminal charges for stalking a former girlfriend.

1985–2000: Mark Ronald Bailey, a New Jersey accountant, sent more than 100 threatening letters to actress Brooke Shields between 1985 and 1999. In September 2000 he was sentenced to 10 years probation, with twice-weekly counseling sessions.

1988–1998: Margaret Ray, a diagnosed schizophrenic, began announcing herself as comedian David Letterman's wife in 1988. She broke into his house at least eight times before committing suicide in 1998.

1988–1990: Tina Ledbetter sent 6,000 threatening letters to actor Michael J. Fox during 1988–90. After Fox took her to court, she began harassing actor Scott Bakula.

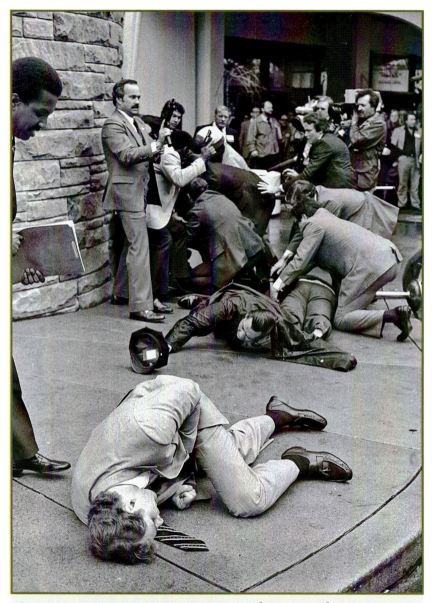

Secret Service agent Timothy J. McCarthy (foreground), Washington policeman Thomas K. Delehanty (center), and press secretary James Brady (background) lie wounded on a street outside a Washington hotel after shots were fired on March 30, 1981, in an attempt to assassinate President Ronald Reagan. The shooter, John Hinckley Jr., is being detained in the background. *Ron Edmonds/AP*

1989: Robert John Bardo shot and killed actress Rebecca Schaeffer outside her Los Angeles home in July 1989, after watching her on television. Police found a "shrine" devoted to Schaeffer in Bardo's apartment. He received a life sentence without parole.

Late 1980s–2001: Gary Benson married an employee of comedian Jerry Lewis in the late 1980s. After they divorced, "voices" told Benson to kill Lewis. He served several jail terms for threatening Lewis and finally died in prison in August 2001.

1987–1990: Joni Leigh Penn sent at least 100 letters to actress Sharon Gless during 1987–89, some including photos of guns. She received a six-year prison term in 1990 after breaking into a house owned by Gless and holding police at bay with a rifle for seven hours.

1988: Nathan Trupp murdered five victims in two states, while stalking actor Michael Landon. Trupp believed Landon was part of a Nazi conspiracy, though in fact, Landon's parents were Jewish. Trupp was confined to a California mental hospital.

1993: Singer Tina Sinatra sued actor James Farentino in 1993 on charges of stalking and threatening her. The court issued a restraining order after Farentino pled "no contest" to the charges.

1995–Present: Robert Hoskins threatened to kill singer Madonna if she refused to marry him. He received a 10-year prison term after invading her estate, armed with a gun, in 1995. Hoskins continues his threats from prison, now claiming that Madonna is his wife.

1997: Ex-convict John Norman tried to invade director Steven Spielberg's estate in June 1997, carrying handcuffs, duct tape, razor blades, and a knife. Norman first identified himself to police as Spielberg's adopted son, then claimed that be believed Spielberg "wanted to be raped by him." Norman received a prison term of 25 years to life in June 1998.

1998–2000: Bernard A. Ortiz received a 10-month jail term in August 1998 for bombarding singer Linda Ronstadt with unwanted cards and letters. Arizona police arrested him again in May 2000 when he violated probation by approaching Ronstadt at a concert.

1999: Athena Marie Rolando invaded actor Brad Pitt's home and played dress-up with his clothes in January 1999. She was sentenced to 15 hours of community service and three years probation.

1999: Barry George shot and killed British TV journalist Jill Dando outside her London home in April 1999. The obsessed fan received a life sentence.

2000: An Internet stalker known only as "Dina" bombarded actress Kate Winslet with frightening e-mails in summer 2000, threatening to "rape her, kill her, and just hit her." The e-mails came from a computer at Aristotle University of Thessalonica, in Greece.

1998–2000: Dante Michael Soiu was committed to a California mental institution in December 2000, with a minimum three-year sentence, for sending actress Gwyneth Paltrow hundreds of unwelcome letters, e-mails, and gifts since 1998.

2000–2001: Matthew Hooker tormented actress Nicole Kidman with letters, love poems, and offers to "tutor" her children between March 2000 and May 2001, when he was slapped with a three-year restraining order. Hooker claims that Kidman "flirted" with him at a bookstore.

2001: Marlon Esracio Pagtakhan received five years probation, with a judicial restraining order, in May 2001, after he pled "no contest" to charges of stalking actress Jeri Ryan (from TV's *Star Trek: Voyager* and *Boston Public*). His harassment of Ryan included "hundreds and hundreds" of threatening e-mails.

2001: Michael Willis faced criminal charges in August 2001, and was held for psychiatric testing, after repeatedly calling actress Katie Holmes's father, asking permission to marry her. Holmes never met Willis, who also demanded $50,000 from NBC network executives, claiming anchorman Tom Brokaw was "stealing" news stories from him.

2002: Juan Carlos Diaz became obsessed with singer Gloria Estefan after playing a small part in one of her music videos. Over the next few months, he stalked Estefan and her husband, while spreading slanderous stories about them. Miami police arrested Diaz in February.

2002: John Hughes, who falsely claims to be actress Meg Ryan's husband, was jailed in Los Angeles during May 2002, after he invaded the property of a Ryan family unrelated to the star. In 2001, he had served six months in prison for carrying three guns on Texas property owned by President George W. Bush.

FIGHTING BACK

While most American stalking victims—an estimated 20,000 persons every year—are not celebrities, the publicity generated by

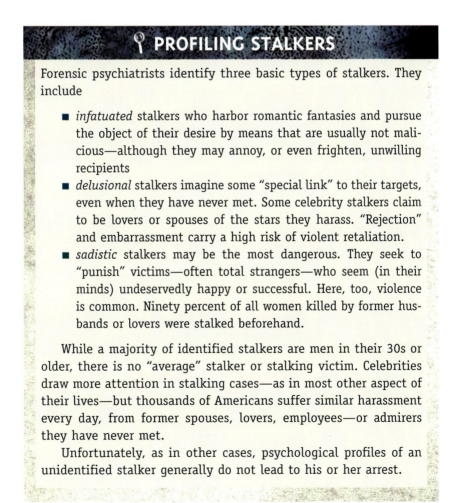

⚲ PROFILING STALKERS

Forensic psychiatrists identify three basic types of stalkers. They include

- *infatuated* stalkers who harbor romantic fantasies and pursue the object of their desire by means that are usually not malicious—although they may annoy, or even frighten, unwilling recipients
- *delusional* stalkers imagine some "special link" to their targets, even when they have never met. Some celebrity stalkers claim to be lovers or spouses of the stars they harass. "Rejection" and embarrassment carry a high risk of violent retaliation.
- *sadistic* stalkers may be the most dangerous. They seek to "punish" victims—often total strangers—who seem (in their minds) undeservedly happy or successful. Here, too, violence is common. Ninety percent of all women killed by former husbands or lovers were stalked beforehand.

While a majority of identified stalkers are men in their 30s or older, there is no "average" stalker or stalking victim. Celebrities draw more attention in stalking cases—as in most other aspect of their lives—but thousands of Americans suffer similar harassment every day, from former spouses, lovers, employees—or admirers they have never met.

Unfortunately, as in other cases, psychological profiles of an unidentified stalker generally do not lead to his or her arrest.

star-stalkers has helped to protect all targets of obsessive love or hate.

Arthur Jackson used California driver's license records to locate actress Theresa Saldana's home in 1982, but her near-murder produced new legislation closing those files to the public. Other states soon followed California's example.

Seven years later, after Robert Bardo stalked and killed actress Rebecca Schaeffer, California passed the first anti-stalking law in American history. Today, all 50 states have similar laws, though procedures and penalties differ. Forty-one states also have laws against cyberstalking by means of computers or other electronic devices. (States without such laws include Idaho, Kentucky, Mississippi, Missouri, Nebraska, New Mexico, Ohio, Utah, and West Virginia.) Interstate transmission of threats via mail, telephone, or other means is also a federal crime.

All stalking victims must follow certain steps to prosecute their tormentors. Acts of harassment must be documented, along with any evidence that may identify the stalker.

Restraining orders, while often ignored by offenders, permit the arrest of a stalker who violates a court's instructions. Second and third arrests also carry more serious penalties than a first offense.

While few noncelebrities can afford bodyguards and security equipment, most local law enforcement agencies today treat stalking as a serious offense with a potential for escalating violence. No victim should suffer in silence.

Let Us Prey

On October 5, 1989, federal jurors in Charlotte, North Carolina, concluded a five-week felony trial by convicting defendant James Orson Bakker on 24 counts of fraud and theft. The case, involving losses of nearly $4 million from various investors, made headlines worldwide. On October 24, the court fined Bakker $500,000 and sentenced him to 45 years in prison.

That sentence might have been routine for a leader of organized crime in New York or Chicago, but James Bakker was no ordinary criminal. In fact, he was a Christian minister, beloved and trusted by tens of thousands around the world—a symbol of religious broadcasting, or televangelism, whose downfall threatened a global network earning millions of dollars each month.

BEFORE THE FALL

A Michigan native, born in 1939, Jim Bakker felt the call of religion in his teens. After high school, he enrolled at North Central Bible College, in Minneapolis, Minnesota. There, he met Tammy Faye LaValley, three years his junior, and they married on April Fools' Day 1961. Ordained as a minister in 1964, Bakker joined Rev. Pat Robertson's small Christian Broadcasting Network in Virginia, pitching in to make its *700 Club* the most successful religious TV program of that time.

In 1974 the Bakkers moved to California, joining televangelists Paul and Jan Crouch to create the new Trinity Broadcasting Network. Soon afterward, Jim and Tammy founded their own PTL Network, variously translated as *Praise the Lord* or *People That Love*. By the early 1980s their *PTL Club* program, broadcast from

Jim and Tammy Faye Bakker talking to their television audience at their PTL Ministry in August 1986. *Lou Krasky/AP*

North Carolina, aired on nearly 100 television stations, claiming more than 12 million daily viewers nationwide. Their Heritage USA Christian theme park, located south of Charlotte, ranked as the third most successful amusement park in America (after Disney World and Disneyland). A state-of-the-art satellite broadcasting system let the Bakkers air their gospel message—and their pleas for money—24 hours a day.

And the money rolled in. Donations from viewers—whom Jim Bakker called "Grandma Grunts"—often exceeded $1 million per week. Although PTL was a nonprofit organization, Jim and Tammy each drew yearly salaries of $200,000, while Jim paid himself more than $4 million in "bonuses" between 1984 and 1987. Their other assets included a $600,000 home and four condominiums in California, a Rolls Royce automobile, and 47 different bank accounts. Their house at Palm Springs had gold-plated bathroom faucets costing $60,000. The Bakkers once spent $100,000 on a private jet to fly their clothes across country. Even their dogs had air-conditioned homes.

Author Frances FitzGerald, writing for the *New Yorker* in April 1987, said that the Bakkers "epitomized the excesses of the 1980s; the greed, the love of glitz, and the shamelessness; which in their case was so pure as to almost amount to a kind of innocence."

But as it turned out, they were not so innocent, after all.

WAGES OF SIN

Extravagant spending was not Jim Bakker's only vice. In December 1980 he had a brief affair with church secretary Jessica Hahn, who later repented and threatened to expose him. Bakker paid Hahn $265,000 in hush money, but she would not stay silent forever.

Threatened with exposure for adultery, Bakker resigned as PTL's president in March 1987. Jessica Hahn posed for *Playboy* magazine, while former colleagues Reverend Jerry Falwell and Reverend Jimmy Swaggart denounced Jim Bakker as a "scab and cancer on the face of Christianity." In April 1987, Reverend John Ankenberg broadened the scandal, accusing Bakker of homosexual activity and stealing millions from PTL. Falwell, meanwhile, took over as PTL's caretaker and quickly ran it into bankruptcy.

The Bakkers denied any wrongdoing, but the tide had turned against them. In May 1987 the Assemblies of God, the Pentecostal denomination to which Bakker belonged, defrocked Jim as a minis-

♀ CELEBRITY SCAMMER

Modern celebrity is both a blessing and a curse. Great wealth and fame bring luxury beyond the imagination to "superstars," but it may also make them targets for a parasitic breed of conartist whose every thought is focused on getting something for nothing. Some stars entrust their cash, their homes—even their lives—to members of an ever-growing entourage who may not always have their best interests at heart.

One such con artist, in the latter 1990s, was celebrity investment counselor Dana Giacchetto, who attached himself to a list of superstars including Ben Affleck, Courtney Cox, Cameron Diaz, Matt Damon, Leonardo DiCaprio, Minnie Driver, Lauren Holly, Jennifer Lopez, Tobey Maguire, Ben Stiller, and even the rock band Phish. Many of the stars who met and befriended Giacchetto trusted him to invest their money, and Giacchetto betrayed that trust.

Not all of his celebrity friends were robbed. A few reported that when their investments went bad Giacchetto repaid them, apparently from his own pocket. In other cases, though, he took advantage of them to turn a tidy profit. Before his final exposure and arrest, Giacchetto stole $33,000 from Ben Affleck, $825,000 from Courtney Cox, $100,000 from Matt Damon, $300,000 from Lauren Holly, $150,000 from Tobey Maguire, $4.7 million from Phish, and $250,000 from Ben Stiller, among many others.

Federal Bureau of Investigation agents launched an investigation of Giacchetto in 1999 and raided his home that November, missing their suspect but seizing crates of documents. Six weeks later, authorities arrested Giacchetto as he returned from a trip to Japan. Prosecutors charged him with stealing more than $9 million from various clients, shuffling money through various accounts to conceal the thefts and support his own lavish lifestyle. Giacchetto's parents bailed him out of jail, but he violated terms of his release in April 2000 by flying to Las Vegas. Police were waiting when he returned to New York—with 80 first-class

ter. On December 5, 1988, federal prosecutors indicted Jim on multiple charges of fraud, tax evasion, and racketeering, claiming that he embezzled some $158 million from the PTL ministry.

airline tickets to various foreign cities, a forged passport, and $4,000 in cash.

Giacchetto pled guilty on five counts of fraud, received a prison term of 57 months, and was ordered to pay $9.9 million in restitution to his victims. The United States Securities Exchange Commission also charged Giacchetto with swindling noncelebrity clients of his now-bankrupt Cassandra Group investment firm and fined him $14.4 million.[1]

Released from custody in July 2003, Giacchetto signed a six-figure publishing deal with Simon & Schuster for his tell-all memoirs, titled *You Will Make Money in Your Sleep*, but attorneys for his victims filed litigation to seize the advance payment. In August 2007 Giacchetto surrendered the book advance, along with any movie, television, or other rights to his story until such time as his victims have been fully repaid for their losses.[2]

Dana Giacchetto, center, leaves the federal courthouse in New York in this April 2000 photo. *Robert Mecea/AP*

According to the government, Bakker and his aides had sold PTL "lifetime memberships" by the tens of thousands between 1984 and 1987, at $1,000 apiece. Each membership entitled its buyer to three nights per year in a luxury hotel at Heritage USA. In fact, only one 500-room hotel was ever built, meaning that most investors never got their money's worth. Bakker kept $3.7 million of the donated cash for himself, while concealing his theft in fraudulent account books.

Bakker's trial began in Charlotte, before Judge Robert Potter, on August 28, 1989. Defense attorneys claimed that Bakker was entitled to profit from his own business, blaming his excesses on poor judgment. Jurors disagreed and convicted Bakker in October, whereupon Judge Potter handed him a 45-year prison sentence. PTL Vice President Richard Dortch also went to prison, for a shorter term.

In early 1991 a federal appeals court upheld Bakker's conviction, but canceled his fine and reduced his prison term to 18 years. Tammy Faye divorced Bakker in 1992. He was paroled to a Salvation Army halfway house in July 1994 after serving less than five years.

BORN AGAIN?

Wealthy evangelist Billy Graham, a longtime friend who bought Bakker a new house and car, eased Bakker's reentry to society. In 1995 Bakker addressed a Christian leadership conference, where 10,000 ministers cheered his speech and gave him a 15-minute standing ovation.

Thus encouraged, Bakker published a book in 1996, in which, despite its title (*I Was Wrong*), Bakker attempted to excuse his prior actions. In print, Bakker claimed that he donated $8 million in personal book royalties to PTL, and that members of PTL's governing board determined all of his income from the ministry, without any pressure from him.

In July 1996 a North Carolina jury dismissed a multimillion-dollar class-action lawsuit filed on behalf of some 160,000 PTL contributors, who donated up to $7,000 each during the 1980s. They would receive no compensation for their losses.

The Internal Revenue Service was less forgiving. After revoking PTL's tax-exempt status, the IRS filed liens against Jim and Tammy Bakker for some $3 million in unpaid income tax. At press time for this book, payments on those debts were continuing.

After divorcing Jim, Tammy Faye married Heritage USA contractor Roe Messner in 1993. (Messner is also subject to an IRS-PTL lien for unpaid taxes.) Both were later diagnosed with different kinds of cancer, crediting a combination of prayer and medicine for their survival into the 21st century. In 1996, Tammy launched a short-lived TV talk show, but poor health forced her to withdraw. She died of cancer in July 2007.

Jim Bakker, meanwhile, returned to televangelism in June 2003, with *The New Jim Bakker Show*. Despite his apparent reform—and admissions that he finished reading the Bible for the first time in prison—some critics remain skeptical of his resurrected faith.

Murder
in Brentwood

Residents of the affluent Brentwood neighborhood in Los Angeles resent disturbances. An example of this was the barking dog that drew attention to a home on South Bundy Drive at 11 p.m. on June 12, 1994. Neighbors investigated, noting that the dog's fur and paws were bloodstained.

Further investigation revealed two bodies sprawled on a nearby path. Both victims had been stabbed and slashed repeatedly. Patrol officers reached the scene at 12:13 a.m., followed by detectives and crime scene investigators.

The victims were identified as 25-year-old Ronald Goldman and 35-year-old Nicole Brown. Brown owned the barking dog and the home where her body was found. Officers recognized her as the ex-wife of athlete and actor O.J. Simpson.

Aside from the corpses, police found a man's knit cap and blood-stained left-hand glove, bloody size-12 footprints, and scattered blood drops suggesting the killer was wounded. At 5 a.m., police went to find Simpson.

THE ALL-AMERICAN

Orenthal James Simpson was born in July 1947. During 1950–53, he suffered from rickets, a bone disease that forced him to wear leg braces. At age 13 he joined a street gang, and was jailed as a juvenile in 1962.

Despite those setbacks, Simpson turned his life around in high school, starring on the football team. At the University of Southern California, he won the Heisman Trophy and a place in the College Football Hall of Fame, twice voted an All-American player.

In 1969 the Buffalo Bills drafted Simpson. He won All-Pro honors five times, and in 1985 became the first Heisman Trophy winner elected to the Pro Football Hall of Fame.

While playing football, Simpson launched a second career as an actor. He played small roles in various TV series (1967–72), then graduated to movies with *Why* (1973), and made 12 more films by 1994.

Ironically, in view of later events, Simpson had his greatest film success playing a detective in the comic *Naked Gun* series (1988–94). Producers considered him for *The Terminator* in 1984, but decided Simpson was "too nice" to play a killer robot.

DOMESTIC TROUBLES

Simpson married high-school girlfriend Marguerite Whitley in 1967. They had three children between 1968 and 1977, then separated after Simpson began an affair with Nicole Brown. Simpson married Nicole Brown in February 1985. Their first child was born eight months later, followed by another in 1988.

In May 1989 Simpson pled "no contest" to charges of beating Nicole. He was sentenced to 120 hours of community service and two years probation. The couple separated in February 1992 and divorced eight months later.

Still, the violence continued. Nicole kept diaries listing 62 incidents of abuse by Simpson. In October 1993 she called police to remove Simpson from her home. After the divorce, she claimed that Simpson threatened to kill her if she ever dated other men.

PRIME SUSPECT

When police reached Simpson's home, a five-minute drive from the murder scene, they found his car parked with its front wheels on the sidewalk. Bloodstains marked the driver's door. Phone calls to the house brought no response for 40 minutes, so officers climbed the wall and rang Simpson's doorbell.

Again, no reply.

In separate bungalows, police found Simpson's oldest daughter and a houseguest, Brian "Kato" Kaelin. Kaelin told officers that he had heard banging sounds behind his bungalow, around 10:45 p.m. Outside, he had met Simpson rushing to a limousine, bound for a late flight to Chicago. Police traced Simpson to his Chicago hotel and informed him of Nicole's murder. Although apparently upset, Simpson asked no questions.

Officer Mark Fuhrman found a bloody right-hand glove behind Kaelin's bungalow. It matched the left glove from the murder scene. Another officer found blood drops leading from Simpson's car, up the driveway to his house.

Police obtained a search warrant for Simpson's home at 11 a.m. Inside, they found a pair of socks in Simpson's bedroom, stained with Nicole's blood. Bloodstains found on and inside Simpson's car matched DNA from both victims.

Simpson arrived while the search was in progress, wearing a bandage on the middle finger of his left hand. Simpson said he had cut his finger before leaving home, then reopened the cut when he broke a glass in Chicago. Police took blood samples and released him.

Autopsy results proved that Brown and Goldman were stabbed with a six-inch knife blade. Police learned that Simpson had purchased a knife of that size, but it was "lost." Detectives never found the murder weapon.

A limousine driver, scheduled to pick Simpson up at 10:30 p.m. on June 12, told police he got no answer on the intercom, but he saw a man of Simpson's size, dressed in dark clothes, run up the driveway at 10:50. Simpson emerged moments later, sweating, and left for the airport. A neighbor confirmed the dark-clad man entering Simpson's estate around 10:45.

On June 17 authorities prepared an arrest warrant for Simpson. Attorney Robert Shapiro agreed to deliver Simpson by 11 a.m., but they never appeared. Police soon learned that Simpson and a friend, Al Cowling, were traveling in a white Ford Bronco. Officers declared Simpson a fugitive at 2 p.m.

At 6:45 p.m. cell phone transmissions led police to the Bronco, cruising aimlessly through Orange County. As squad cars closed in, Cowling dialed 911 and told police that Simpson was suicidal, holding a gun to his head. News helicopters broadcast the "slow-speed chase" worldwide until Simpson surrendered at 8:45 p.m. An estimated 95 million TV viewers watched the event from start to finish.

Simpson hired a team of high-priced lawyers to defend him. Aside from Shapiro, the stars of the team included celebrity attorney F. Lee Bailey, flamboyant former prosecutor Johnnie Cochran, and DNA expert Barry Scheck.

The booking mug shot for O.J. Simpson taken on June 17, 1994, after he surrendered to authorities at his Brentwood estate in Los Angeles. Simpson was charged with two counts of murder in connection with the slayings of his ex-wife, Nicole Brown, and acquaintance Ron Goldman. *AP/Los Angeles Police Department*

Against that team stood prosecutor Marcia Clark and her assistant, Christopher Darden. Judge Lance Ito would preside over the televised Simpson trial, in full view of a massive TV audience.

TRIAL OF THE CENTURY

Simpson's trial, beginning on January 24, 1995, was closely watched by millions. Some 2,000 reporters covered the story, while video feeds carried the live action to the world at large. The *Los Angeles Times* alone published more than 1,000 articles on Simpson's case.

At any given time during the trial's 133 days, 91 percent of America's TV audience watched the trial in progress. An incredible 150 million watched or listened on radio when jurors finally delivered their verdict. Talk show host Larry King told his CNN viewers, "If we had God booked and O.J. was available, we'd move God."

The prosecution's case was simple. They claimed Simpson was a violent, possessive man who beat Nicole while they were married and threatened her life if she dated after their divorce. Finally, he carried out his threats.

The defense presented conspiracy theories, claiming that racist police framed Simpson because he was black and the victims were white. They accused various detectives of planting evidence and faking DNA test results.

During eight months of trial, 150 witnesses testified before the Simpson jury. Experts spent weeks on the DNA evidence, while footprint specialists matched crime scene tracks to a pair of expensive Bruno Magli shoes in Simpson's size. The shoes were missing, and Simpson denied owning any, but photos showed him wearing them shortly before the murders.

Defense attorneys grilled the prosecution's experts on their handling of scientific evidence, charging that police used Simpson's blood to fake crime scene evidence. They noted that one spot of Simpson's blood was not collected from the murder scene until July 3, three weeks after the killings.

Over time, the jury became confused. Foreperson Amanda Cooley later told reporters, "Witness after witness, day after day, they lost us. When we went on a break, everybody heaved a sigh of relief."

Jurors paid attention, though, when prosecutors asked Simpson to try on the bloody murder gloves. Nicole bought Simpson two pairs of the same brand in 1990, and photos showed him wearing them. However, when Simpson donned the gloves in court (over another pair of latex gloves), they were too small.

Prosecutors argued that the gloves had shrunk from exposure to water. When Simpson tried on a new pair—same size, without rubber gloves underneath—they fit perfectly. Still, Johnnie Cochran told jurors, "If it doesn't fit, you must acquit."

⚲ REAL-LIFE CSI: DNA

DNA profiling is widely regarded as the last word in personal identification. According to experts, the odds against two different people matching the same complete DNA profile are 100 *billion* to one. Earth's population in 2006 was about 6.5 billion. In the Simpson case, O.J.'s bloodstain at the Brentwood crime scene matched only one person in 57 billion—more than nine times Earth's total population. It could be no one else's. So, how could the jury acquit him?

Four theories explain the outcome:

1. *Ignorance.* After the trial, prosecutor Marcia Clark described the jurors as "moon rocks." One juror, who admittedly read nothing but horse-racing forms and "didn't really understand" those, told reporters, "I didn't understand the DNA stuff at all. To me, it was a waste of time."

2. *Conspiracy.* Some jurors may have believed defense arguments that police framed Simpson. However, it is physically impossible to make an unknown killer's DNA match that of another person. In order to accept the conspiracy theory, the DNA evidence must be overlooked.

3. *Incompetent prosecutors.* Raised by Charles Manson prosecutor Vincent Bugliosi and others, this theory suggests that the district attorney's office bungled its presentation of critical evidence so badly that the jurors could not understand it.

4. *Jury nullification.* This term describes a jury verdict that ignores the facts to make a point. In Simpson's case, some observers believe that the jury, dominated by African Americans, acquitted Simpson to "punish" Los Angeles police for past mistreatment of minorities.[1]

And so they did, on October 3, 1995. Despite the state's "mountain of evidence," the jurors found Simpson not guilty.

That verdict was highly controversial—a reaction mirrored in 80-plus books and thousands of articles published about the case since 1995.

Simpson welcomed the verdict—but he still had other trials to face.

JUSTICE AT LAST?

While Simpson was cleared of criminal charges, relatives of Nicole and Ron Goldman filed a civil lawsuit charging him with wrongful death of their loved ones. That trial began on October 23, 1996, with some important differences.

First, civil trials do not require proof "beyond a reasonable doubt," merely a "preponderance of the evidence." Second, a majority of jurors in the second trial were affluent Caucasians, while most of the juror's in Simpson's criminal case were African Americans. Both of these factors led to a different type of trial.

On February 4, 1997, the new jury found Simpson responsible for killing both victims. They could not send him to jail, but they ordered him to pay the Brown and Goldman families $33.5 million.

Simpson's lawyer told the court his client was penniless, unable to pay the judgment. In fact, Simpson receives $4 million yearly from a pension fund created during his football career, but that money was deemed untouchable.

After the civil trial, Simpson moved with his two youngest children to a $1.5 million home in Florida. There, he told reporters, "It will be a cold day in hell before I pay a penny."

He never has.

ALTERNATE THEORIES

During and after Simpson's murder trial, various theories were offered naming alternate suspects. They include

- *A hitman.* This story claims that a professional assassin, hired by drug dealers whom Brown and her friends had failed to pay for cocaine, killed Brown and Goldman. Nicole's best friend was an admitted addict, and Al Cowlings once worked as a bodyguard for a notorious drug smuggler who escaped from jail three weeks before the killings.

- *Glenn Rogers.* A serial killer, convicted of murders in several states, Rogers painted Nicole's home in January 1994 and later bragged to friends about the killings. Police have found no evidence linking Rogers to the crimes.
- *Jason Simpson.* Author William Dear, in his book *O.J. is Guilty, but Not of Murder* (2000), names Simpson's oldest son as the killer. Dear claims Jason—who pled "no contest" to another assault charge in 1993—had a crush on Nicole but resented her "swinging" lifestyle. After the murders, Dear claims O.J. concealed evidence to protect his son.
- *Kato Kaelin.* After Simpson's trial, a tabloid newspaper named Kaelin as a suspect. He sued for $15 million and later settled out of court for an undisclosed amount.

AFTERMATH

Trouble continues to haunt O.J. Simpson. At last report, Florida police had answered four domestic dispute calls involving Simpson and his latest girlfriend, but they filed no charges.

On December 4, 2000, Simpson became embroiled in a "road rage" incident, allegedly attacking Miami motorist Jeffrey Pattinson. Police charged Simpson with assault and battery, but jurors acquitted him in October 2001.

Still, the publicity continues. In one interview, discussing Nicole's death, Simpson mimed stabbing with a banana and mimicked the shrill theme from *Psycho.* His pay-per-view comedy special (*Juiced,* 2003) drew criticism for a sketch where Simpson tries to sell his alleged murder car to a used-car dealer, saying, "It was good for me. It helped me get away."

Others involved in the case also staked a claim to fame. Polls from 1995 showed that 74 percent of Americans recognized Kato Kaelin, while only 25 percent knew Vice President Al Gore. Kaelin pursued that notoriety as a radio talk-show host and in various TV appearances through 2005.

Prosecutors Marcia Clark and Christopher Darden both published books about the Simpson trial. Clark later became a reporter for *Entertainment Tonight*. Darden published a successful novel, *The Trials of Nikki Hill*, in 1999.

In 2006 Simpson authored *If I Did It*, a fictional account of the murders written as if he had committed them. Unprecedented negative reaction from the public led the publisher to cancel the book, and a Florida court then awarded the publication rights to the Goldman family as partial payment of the amount awarded in their civil case against Simpson. The book was published with comments added by the Goldmans in September 2007, under the title *If I Did It: Confessions of the Killer*.

Also in September 2007, Simpson landed back in trouble with the law for his alleged role in a Las Vegas robbery. Simpson and several accomplices were arrested and accused of taking memorabilia from a room in the Palace Station hotel. In November Simpson was charged with numerous felonies in connection to the case, ranging from assault with a deadly weapon to conspiracy to commit kidnapping. He awaits trial as of this writing.

OFF-FIELD CRIMES

The Simpson case also highlighted the sad truth that star athletes are just as affected by crime as any other kind of celebrities. Top players in all sports have committed crimes, been connected to criminal activity, or become victims at the hands of criminals.

The most notorious scandal in baseball history occurred at the 1919 World Series when eight Chicago White Sox players purposely lost the series against the Cincinnati Reds. Mob fixer Arnold Rothstein arranged for the players to be paid $100,000 to assure the loss so that gamblers could place sure bets on the winning team. When the scandal broke, the team earned the nickname "Chicago Black Sox," and newly appointed baseball commissioner Judge Kenesaw Mountain Landis banned all eight players from baseball for life.

Gambling reared its ugly head again in the 1980s, when it was learned that baseball's all-time hits leader, Pete Rose, gambled on Cincinnati Reds games while he was the team's manager. Rose agreed to a voluntary lifetime ban from baseball, and the scandal has haunted him ever since. But there were other problems with baseball in the 1980s, including widespread cocaine abuse, which

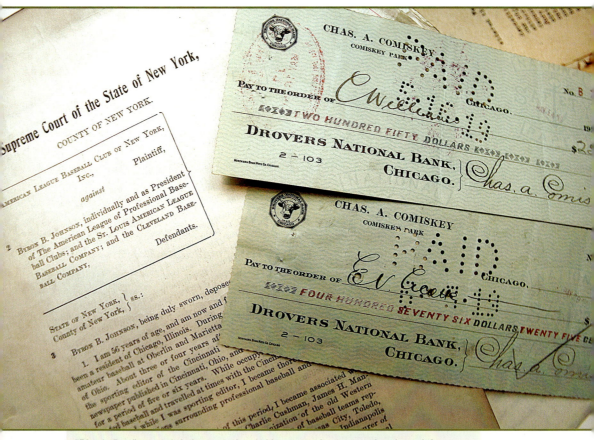

"Black Sox" scandal documents, letters, and memos displayed for an auction. The items were sold to the Chicago History Museum for $100,000. *Nam Y. Huh/AP*

wound up hitting the Pittsburgh Pirates the hardest. Several Pirates players testified in court and were penalized for their drug abuse.

Drugs of a different kind continue to cast a shadow on Major League Baseball: steroids. Use of these banned, performance-enhancing drugs have been an issue since the early 1990s. Allegations of steroid use have tainted the home run records of Mark McGwire, Sammy Sosa, and Barry Bonds. Allegations continue today, and investigations into steroid use are ongoing as of this writing.

In the boxing world, Mike Tyson stands out as one athlete whose life has been as violent outside the ring as it has been inside it. Convicted of rape in 1992, Tyson served three years in prison before resuming his boxing career. In 1997 Tyson was disqualified during a match with Evander Holyfield after he bit off part of Holyfield's ear. The two-time heavyweight champ ran afoul of the law again in 1999, with a conviction for assault, and he pled guilty on drug charges in 2007. Despite his criminal record, Tyson remains a widely popular, if very controversial, athlete.

Among gridiron gladiators, Baltimore Ravens Ray Lewis and Jamal Lewis (no relation) have had run-ins with the law. Ray Lewis was accused of murder in 2000 but accepted a plea bargain that sentenced him to one year probation in return for testifying against others involved. In 2005 another Ravens player, Jamal Lewis, was sentenced to four months in jail for his role in a drug deal. In 2007 Atlanta Falcons quarterback Michael Vick was at the heart of a scandal involving dog fighting. Vick eventually pled guilty and was sentenced to jail time.

On the flip side, Washington Redskins player Sean Taylor became a crime victim when he was murdered after interrupting a burglary in his Miami home. Taylor, age 24, was an up-and-coming player, known for his aggressive playing style. As of this writing, his murder remains unsolved.

On the basketball court, rape charges sullied the reputation of widely popular, star shooting guard Kobe Bryant. Drafted into the National Basketball Association straight from high school, Bryant had a reputation as a clean-cut player until 2003, when a woman accused him of sexual assault. Bryant maintained that his encounter with the woman was consensual but ultimately made an undisclosed financial settlement with the woman, after which charges were dropped. During the controversy, Bryant lost several lucrative endorsement contracts, and some commentators theorized that the woman had targeted Bryant because of his celebrity, though that was never proven.

Number One with a Bullet

On September 7, 1996, a boxing match between Mike Tyson and Bruce Sheldon drew many celebrities to the MGM Grand Hotel in Las Vegas, Nevada. Members of the audience included hip-hop music star Tupac Shakur and Marion "Suge" Knight, owner of hip-hop label Death Row Records.

After the main event, Shakur met Orlando Anderson, a member of the Crips street gang, in the hotel lobby. Anderson had beaten one of Shakur's bodyguards a few weeks earlier, and now Shakur got even, knocking Anderson down and watching while his entourage stomped him. The fight was caught on videotape.

From the MGM, Shakur and Knight drove toward Club 662, owned by Death Row. Before they reached it, at 11:14 p.m., another car pulled alongside and sprayed Knight's vehicle with bullets. Four shots struck Shakur, missing the large "Thug Life" tattoo across his stomach.

Shakur survived for six days at a local hospital, then died on September 13. He was 25 years old, and his murder remains unsolved—a symbol of the violence that surrounds rap music in America.

"GANGSTA" ART

In hip-hop (or rap) music most lyrics are spoken or chanted, rather than sung to a melody, and musical accompaniment often consists of samples taken from existing songs, often from other musical genres, such as pop, rock, and rhythm and blues. Hip-hop

Rapper Tupac Shakur, left, and Death Row Records Chairman Marion "Suge" Knight in August 1996. Shakur died on September 13, 1996, the victim of a drive-by shooting. His murder remains unsolved. *Frank Wiese/AP*

music emerged among New York City's African-American population in the 1970s. The first successful rap albums were released in 1979, after which rap's popularity spread nationwide, and it went on to become a cultural phenomenon in the 1980s and 1990s. Despite its commercial success, some critics noted that much hip-hop music celebrates the crime and violence of "gangsta" life.

Suge Knight and partner Dr. Dre founded Death Row Records in 1991, soon becoming a dominant force on the hip-hop scene. Much of their funding came from an imprisoned drug dealer called Harry-O. Some headline performers, including white rapper Vanilla Ice, also claimed that Knight illegally used their money to launch the new label.

Tension soon sparked between Death Row and rival Bad Boy Entertainment, owned by Sean "Puffy" Combs.

That feud was only one of several hip-hop battles brewing by the early 1990s. Death Row's Tupac Shakur and Bad Boy rapper Notorious B.I.G. were outspoken enemies, while a state of near-war existed between rappers on the East and West Coasts of the United States. Assaults and shootings were almost routine by 1996, when Shakur made his fateful trip to Las Vegas.

Meanwhile, critics complained that gangsta rap promoted drugs, abuse of women, and murder. Fans of the music replied that hip-hop was no more harmful, for its time, than the Beatles or Rolling Stones were in the 1960s. But the rising death toll indicated that they might have been wrong.

2PACALYPSE

Tupac Shakur was born into the thug life that he sang about, in June 1971. A child of New York City's Harlem neighborhood, he was one year old when police framed his godfather—black militant Elmer "Geronimo" Pratt—on false murder charges in Los Angeles. Fourteen years later, his stepfather Mutulu Shakur received a life sentence for an armored car robbery in which two policemen were killed.

Tupac's family moved to California in 1988, and he launched his show business career as a backup dancer in 1990. A year later, he released his first rap album, *2Pacalypse Now*. A second album followed in 1993, while Shakur showed a new side to his talent in various movie roles. In 1993 he formed the group Thug Life to produce more albums, but trouble haunted him.

In 1991 Shakur sued Oakland police, alleging that officers brutalized him for jaywalking. The department settled his $10 million claim for $42,000. In October 1993 Shakur shot two off-duty Atlanta policemen, but charges were dropped when he proved both officers were drunk and carrying stolen guns. In 1994 Shakur received a 15-day sentence for assaulting a former employer.

Jurors convicted Shakur of sexual assault in 1995, resulting in a four-year prison term. The day before that verdict, he suffered five gunshot wounds at a Manhattan recording studio. He later blamed Sean Combs and the Notorious B.I.G. for that attack. Paroled after 11 months, Shakur faced a lawsuit from parents of a child killed in a

♀ THUG LIFE

Tupac Shakur's famous "Thug Life" tattoo fairly describes the behavior of some other hip-hop celebrities. A partial list of those in trouble with the law includes

- Marion "Suge" Knight, co-founder of Death Row records. Throughout his career, charges of violence and gang affiliations have followed Knight. Various Death Row performers (including Snoop Dogg and Vanilla Ice) accused him of assaulting them, while some conspiracy theories implicate Knight in the deaths of Tupac and Biggie Smalls, as well as other murders. Knight received probation for weapons and assault charges in 1992, then got nine years in prison for violating probation in 1996. Released in 2001, he served 61 days for violating parole in December 2002. In July 2003 he received a 10-month sentence for assault. In August 2005 he paid a fine for drug possession. A few days later, in Miami, Knight was wounded in a drive-by shooting.
- Gerard "D.O. Cannon" Fields, a New York City rapper, was killed by unknown gunman on August 9, 2003. Four days earlier, a friend of rapper 50 Cent was shot dead near the same location.

1992 shootout involving Tupac's entourage. Shakur settled that case for an estimated $500,000.

At the end of his life, Shakur was recognized as one of America's foremost rap artists, with plans for a film production company and a new drink called Thug Passion. His time ran out before he realized those dreams, leaving the question: Who shot Tupac?

NOTORIOUS

Some investigators blamed the Crips, retaliating for Shakur's beating of Orlando Anderson, but others focused on rival rapper Christopher Wallace, known professionally as the Notorious B.I.G. or Biggie Smalls. Wallace denied involvement in the crime, noting that

- Cordozar "Snoop Dogg" Broadus, a renowned west coast rapper, faced trial as an accessory to murder in 1993. Jurors acquitted him but convicted his bodyguard. In April 2006, Broadus and several friends were jailed in London for starting a brawl at Heathrow Airport. Although released without trial, Broadus was banned from England.
- Sean "Puffy" Combs, founder of Bad Boy Records, stood accused of assaulting a rival producer in April 1999. Eight months later, Combs and a friend were jailed on weapons charges after a New York shooting. Jurors later acquitted him. Media reports in 2004 claimed Combs was friendly with members of the Gambino Mafia family.
- Marshall "Eminem" Mathers, America's leading white rapper, holds numerous Grammies and an Academy Award for his film *8 Mile* (2002). In June 2000 he allegedly pistol-whipped his ex-wife's boyfriend, later pleading guilty to weapons possession while assault charges were dropped. Mathers received two years probation and paid a $100,000 fine. A similar incident, involving rival rapper Douglas Dail of the Insane Clown Posse, earned Mathers another year on probation in 2001.

he was in New York when Shakur was shot, but Tupac's friends claimed that Biggie hired the gunmen. A friend of Shakur's who said he could identify the shooters was later shot by unknown killers in New Jersey.

Wallace was born in Brooklyn's Bedford-Stuyvesant neighborhood in 1972. He turned to music after serving 10 months in jail for selling cocaine and released his first album, *Ready to Die,* in 1994. Within a year, the Notorious B.I.G. ranked among the nation's

The bullet-sprayed passenger door of the GMC Suburban in which rapper the Notorious B.I.G. was riding when he was shot. The 24-year-old, whose real name was Christopher Wallace, was pronounced dead at a local hospital shortly after the shooting. *Mike Meadows/AP*

best-known rappers. Friends called him "King of New York," after a gangster film released in 1990.

Despite his critical success, B.I.G. was best known for his role in rap's East–West feud of the 1990s. His personal quarrels with Tupac Shakur highlighted the rivalry between Bad Boy and Death Row groups nationwide. Despite a friendly meeting at the 1996 MTV Music Awards, many critics still blamed B.I.G. for Tupac's murder.

At 1 a.m. on March 9, 1997, while leaving a party in Los Angeles, Wallace was ambushed and shot six times in his car. He died almost instantly, while the drive-by shooters escaped. His murder, like Shakur's, remains officially unsolved, but early suspicion focused on Suge Knight and his alleged street-gang associates. Another theory blames the Crips, claiming that Wallace failed to pay them for their service as his bodyguards.

"DEATH IS A COMMODITY"

Sudden death only increased the fame and fortune of Tupac Shakur and Biggie Smalls, though neither man was able to enjoy it. B.I.G.'s second album, *Life After Death,* was released two weeks after his murder and debuted at No. 1 on the charts.

Employees at the Greenwich Village Tower Records outlet told the Associated Press that they sold 105 copies of *Life After Death* in its first hour. "It's flying out of here," one said. "Death is a commodity, you know. I have to keep stocking it every five minutes."

Cashing in on the trend, a car-rental company announced that they would sell the bullet-punctured door of the vehicle in which Smalls died. It was for charity, they said, with any proceeds going to the Challenger Boys & Girls Club of South Central Los Angeles. The asking price: $4,000.

Tupac Shakur, in death, has been treated with somewhat greater respect. In 2003, MTV's countdown of "22 Greatest MCs" listed Shakur in the top position. A year later, *VIBE* magazine readers voted him "the greatest rapper of all time." In 2005, his album *The Don Kiluminati: The 7 Day Theory* took MTV honors as one of the Top 10 Greatest Hip-Hop Albums of All Time. A year later, MTV ranked Shakur second among its Top 10 MCs of All Time.

Fate has not been so kind to Suge Knight, who filed for bankruptcy in April 2006. Lydia Harris, an investor who owned 50 percent of Death Row Records, claimed that Knight had cheated her out of $107 million. A court agreed, but bankruptcy makes it unlikely that Harris will see any cash.

Sean Combs, meanwhile, rides the wave of success, listed by *Fortune* magazine in 2002 as one of America's "40 Richest People Under 40." Expanding beyond Bad Boy Entertainment, Combs now owns a movie production company, a restaurant chain, and his own clothing line.

Sticky Fingers

The Saks Fifth Avenue department store on Wilshire Boulevard in Beverly Hills, California, caters to wealthy shoppers. Its prices are high, and many of its customers spend thousands of dollars per visit.

Others hope to get the goods for free.

On December 12, 2001, Saks security guards manned their closed-circuit monitors, tracking a pretty young woman as she toured the store, stuffing various expensive items into shopping bags, putting on a hat, draping her arms with designer outfits. She slipped into a changing room, then emerged to purchase items valued at $3,700.

Guards met her at the exit, checked her bulging bags, and found another $5,500 worth of stolen merchandise inside. They took her into custody and called police. Some of them may have recognized their prisoner. She was Winona Ryder, star of 25 movies in the past 15 years, twice nominated for Academy Awards.

GIRL, INTERRUPTED

Ryder was born Winona Horowitz in 1971, named for her hometown of Winona, Minnesota. Part of her childhood was spent in a California "hippie" commune, where her parents befriended LSD guru Timothy Leary. In junior high school, harassment by ignorant bullies who mistook her for a skinny boy prompted Winona's parents to try homeschooling.

Ryder auditioned for her first film role at age 14, and while she missed that part, she signed to play Rina in the movie *Lucas* one year later. The *Los Angeles Times* called her next role, in the dark comedy *Heathers* (1987), "a remarkable debut," and Ryder was well on her way to success.

More roles followed, including *Beetlejuice* (1988), *Edward Scissorhands* (1990), and *Bram Stoker's Dracula* (1992). Ryder received her first Golden Globe nomination in 1991, for *Mermaids.* Three years later, she won that award and received an Oscar nomination for Best Supporting Actress for her performance in *The Age of Innocence.* In 1995 she received another Oscar nomination, this time for Best Actress, for *Little Women.*

Despite rave reviews, Ryder missed an Oscar nod for her starring role in *Girl, Interrupted* (1999), the story of a young psychiatric patient, which she also produced, while costar Angelina Jolie won an Academy Award for Best Supporting Actress. In October 2000 Ryder received a star in her name on Hollywood's Walk of Fame—an honor for which celebrities pay $15,000 to the Hollywood Historic Trust.

Ryder seemed unstoppable—until the news from Saks made global headlines in 2001.

ARREST AND TRIAL

When first detained, Ryder told security guards that the director of her latest film told her to steal, as preparation for her role. At first, she claimed the film's title was *Shopgirl,* then changed it to *White Jazz.* (As it turned out, there was no such film.) When that argument failed, she offered to charge the items on her credit card, along with the $3,700 already spent, but store employees refused.

Witnesses told police they had watched Ryder cut the tags from various expensive items, stuffing the tags into pockets of a coat she left in the store. She cut herself in the process, leaving bloodstains on one of her bags. The stolen items included a $1,500 Gucci dress, a $525 Dolce & Gabbana purse, and an $80 pair of cashmere socks. Police also found a bottle of narcotic painkillers in Ryder's purse, for which she carried no prescription.

District Attorney Stephen Cooley assigned eight prosecutors to Ryder's case, filed four felony charges, and demanded that her trial be televised. Critics called the proceeding a politically motivated "show trial," noting that Cooley had accepted more than 5,000 misdemeanor plea bargains in similar cases since 1999, but denied the same offer to Ryder.

Various delays postponed Ryder's trial, including a June 2002 incident in which she collided with a television film crew outside the courtroom and fractured her arm. On October 9, 2002, prosecutors dropped their drug charge against Ryder, when her doctor confirmed writing the prescription.

Ryder's trial for burglary, grand theft, and vandalism finally began on October 23, 2002. Prosecutors played the Saks security

Actress Winona Ryder listens as the verdict is read in her shoplifting trial on November 6, 2002. *Lee Celano/AP*

videotapes and called witnesses to describe Ryder's actions. On November 6 jurors acquitted her of burglary, but convicted her on the other two charges. Ryder received a sentence of three years probation, 480 hours of community service, and a $10,055 fine.

Despite the media hype surrounding Ryder's case, she served no jail time. On June 18, 2004, an appeals court reduced her charges to misdemeanors.

The scandal interrupted Ryder's promising career. She appeared in two films during 2002, then took a two-year break before her next movie, in 2004. She appeared in several films released in 2006 and 2007, with others scheduled for 2008, suggesting that the incident did not damage her career in the long term.

WANT VS. NEED

Ryder is not the only celebrity who has been caught stealing items she could easily afford. Far from it. In June 2006 the NNDB Web site (www.nndb.com) listed 35 famous actors, musicians, and athletes whose public records feature shoplifting charges. A sampling includes

- Actress Farrah Fawcett, twice arrested during 1970. Both charges were reduced to trespassing. She paid $390 in fines.
- Musician Courtney Love, who took a T-shirt from Woolworth's in 1978.
- Imelda Marcos, former first lady of the Philippines, who stole hundreds of millions with her husband Fernando, then hid in the United States to avoid prosecution during 1986–89. Store cameras caught her stealing buttons from designer clothing in a posh department store, but no charges were filed.
- John Shannon, Secretary of the Army under President Bill Clinton, charged with stealing women's clothing on an army base in August 1993.
- Tennis star Jennifer Capriati, held for stealing jewelry in December 1993. She first called it an "accident," then told authorities she felt "so fat and ugly" that she wanted to die. Capriati also faced drug charges in May 1994 and entered voluntary treatment.
- Olympic gymnast Olga Korbut, arrested for stealing $19 worth of groceries from a Georgia market in January 2002. She paid a $300 fine four months later.

- Country singer Lynn Anderson, arrested in January 2005 for stealing a Harry Potter DVD in New Mexico. Previously, Anderson was jailed on drunk-driving charges.

FIVE-FINGER DISCOUNTS

According to the Los Angeles County District Attorney's office, more than 10 percent of all Americans are guilty of shoplifting. Juvenile offenders make up 25 percent of that total, and retailers lose more than $20 billion to theft every year.

♀ TO CATCH A THIEF

Winona Ryder's case illustrates the modern methods used to catch shoplifters. First, she was observed for 90 minutes with closed-circuit security cameras that followed her around the store and recorded her actions for later use in court. Security guards who had watched her also testified at Ryder's trial. The merchandise recovered from her bags without receipts was evidence of theft. Bloodstains on one of her shopping bags—an unusual aspect in theft cases—also supported eyewitness descriptions of Ryder removing price tags.

In order to convict a shoplifter, the prosecutor must prove several points. Those include

- *Actual theft.* A theft is not complete until the shoplifter carries merchandise out of a store without paying for it. Hasty arrests inside the store generally will not support conviction, regardless of suspicious circumstances. The thief must be caught outside the store with stolen items physically in his or her possession.
- *Intent to steal.* A theft must be deliberate, rather than accidental. Shoppers without carts or baskets, who place small items in a purse or pocket while browsing, may later argue that they honestly forgot to pay for certain merchandise. Charges filed in such cases are sometimes thrown out of court, especially when the defendant is a first-time offender.

(continues)

(continued)

- *Title to property*. Prosecutors must prove that merchandise was stolen from the shop in question, not carried into the store by a shopper who purchased it elsewhere. Any person might conceivably carry a book, jewelry, small tools, or cosmetics into stores selling those items, and then be arrested for theft while leaving. In such cases, proof is supplied by price or security tags, and by the size or unique nature of the merchandise. (For example, no rational person would hide a brand-new chainsaw underneath his coat to carry it inside a hardware store.)

Even when all those elements are present, exclusive stores catering to celebrities may not prosecute millionaire thieves. The Internet is rife with anecdotal tales from shopkeepers in Hollywood and elsewhere describing anonymous movie stars and other famous folk who routinely shoplift for "kicks." In some cases, the shoplifter's manager or publicity agent allegedly pays the bills. Other thieves are deterred by the close attention of sales personnel. Some sticky-fingered celebs reportedly escape punishment because their victims fear bad publicity and loss of wealthy clients, because prosecution costs more than the items stolen (which, in most cases, are covered by the store's insurance), or because of the demands on store personnel who must appear in court.

Jack L. Hayes International, a security consulting firm, puts the statistics even higher. During 2004 alone, Hayes reports, security guards for 27 large retail chains caught 752,629 shoplifters stealing merchandise valued above $441 billion from 12,908 stores. The average shoplifter stole items worth $150 in a single outing. (Meanwhile, 63,289 dishonest employees stole an average of $671 each in the same year.)

Some shoplifters are professional thieves, operating in teams to distract store employees. Others steal to feed their drug habits, while some only pretend to shoplift, hoping they can later sue the store for false arrest. Meanwhile, increasing numbers of "normal" people—including the rich and famous—apparently steal for the thrill of it.

Psychologists describe compulsive theft (*kleptomania*) as a form of mental illness or addiction, but most American courts do not allow insanity pleas in shoplifting cases since motive is deemed irrelevant.

Penalties for shoplifting generally depend on the value of merchandise stolen, the defendant's age, and the number of prior offenses. State laws establish monetary limits for petty theft (a misdemeanor) and grand theft (a felony). Generally, misdemeanors are punished by fines, probation, community service, and/or a maximum of 12 months in county jail. Felonies involve state prison terms and larger fines.

First-time offenders are usually treated more leniently than defendants with multiple arrests. The normal first-offense shoplifting charge in Los Angeles involves a small fine, community service, and one to three years probation. For that reason, many critics regarded the D.A.'s filing of felony charges against Winona Ryder as a publicity stunt.

A Shot in the Dark

Studio City, located 12 miles northwest of downtown Los Angeles, is named for the movie studios that built their headquarters there in the 1920s. With 30,000 residents and many stylish shops, it is sometimes called the "Jewel of the San Fernando Valley." But crime presents a danger, even there.

On the evening of May 4, 2001, actor Robert Blake took his wife of six months to dinner at a restaurant on Tujunga Boulevard, in Studio City. Blake parked his car on nearby Woodbridge Street, beneath a burned-out streetlight, and the couple walked arm-in-arm to the restaurant, two blocks away. They lingered over dinner and drinks until 9:35 p.m.

Blake later told police that they were halfway to the car when he discovered that he had left his licensed pistol in their restaurant booth. He went back to fetch it while Bonnie went on to the car. Returning moments later with the gun, Blake found his wife slumped over in her seat, bleeding from a head wound.

Blake tried to revive her, then ran to the nearby home of a friend, filmmaker Sean Stanek, ringing the doorbell and pleading for help. Stanek later described Blake weeping and vomiting. Blake and Stanek ran back to Blake's car at 9:50, and then Blake rushed to the restaurant in search of medical aid. A nurse among the diners left her meal and found Blake's wife barely alive, unable to speak.

A phone call brought police and an ambulance racing to the scene, where officers discovered that Blake's wife had been shot once, behind her right ear. She died soon afterward, at a local hospital, without regaining consciousness.

Blake gave a tearful statement to police, explaining that he carried a gun because his wife had feared someone was stalking her.

Detectives listened, unaware that this case would become another classic mystery of Hollywood.

A TROUBLED STAR

Robert Blake was a second-generation Italian American, born Michael Gubitosi in September 1933. His parents performed as a song-and-dance team, billing their children as "The Three Little Hillbillies." In 1938 they left New Jersey for California, where all three children worked as movie extras. Michael—billed as "Mickey"—had the most success, but there was also much to overcome.

In later years, Blake told reporters that his parents were "committably insane," describing his father as a "sadistic maniac" and his home as "a very diseased, terrible household." According to Blake, he was frequently locked in a closet, forced to eat off the floor, often beaten, and sexually abused. By the time Blake's father killed himself in 1955, Michael was well established as a Hollywood child star.

He began working steadily in 1939, as "Little Mickey" in MGM's *Our Gang* comedy features. He filmed 39 episodes in that series over the next five years, changing his screen name to Bobby Blake in 1943. Blake also made 53 other films between 1939 and 1950, including portrayal of "Little Beaver" in 22 episodes of the *Red Ryder* series, for Republic Pictures. His dark hair and complexion often saw Blake cast as a Mexican or Native American character.

Blake joined the army in 1950 and served in Alaska, where he fell in love for the first time. In later interviews, he admitted acting "like a madman" and plotting to kill the girl's father, who opposed their relationship.

Back in civilian life, Blake resumed his former acting career and stayed busy, filming 24 movies and 43 television series episodes between 1952 and 1974. Seventeen of those roles required him to play Hispanic or Native American characters. Blake also frequently portrayed detectives or criminals, earning critical praise for his performance as a real-life mass-murderer in the film *In Cold Blood* (1967).

Throughout those busy years, Blake harbored suicidal thoughts and sought help from psychiatrists. He married actress Sondra Kerr in 1964 and fathered two children before he and Kerr divorced in

1983. Blake later described their marriage as "a 14-carat disaster," featuring "terrible, sick fights." Sondra told friends that Blake was obsessively jealous and frequently threatened to kill her. She told tabloid reporters that when they divorced, Blake "terrorized" her into granting him full custody of their children.

Before all that, Blake landed his signature role as a tough, wise-cracking cop on the TV series *Baretta* (1975–78). When that program folded, Blake made 13 more films between 1980 and 1997. Another short-lived TV series, *Hell Town* (1985), cast Blake as a priest fighting crime and sin in a tough neighborhood.

Blake's career ranked as one of the longest in Hollywood history. And then he met Bonnie.

THE CON ARTIST

Bonnie Lee Bakley (1956–2001) was born in New Jersey. She quit school at 16 to become an actress and model, but failed at both pursuits. Instead, she drifted into crime, logging convictions for drug offenses (1989), check fraud (1995), and possessing false identification (1998). Her main con was a "lonely-hearts" scam, wherein she offered love and nude photos to men who sent her money.

Bakley was also obsessed with celebrities, claiming friendships and romantic affairs with many famous men, including some she never met. Some called her a stalker. (A DNA test disproved her claim that rock legend Jerry Lee Lewis fathered one of her children in 1993.) With eight failed marriages behind her, Bakley was dating actor Marlon Brando's son in 1999, when she met Robert Blake.

While dating both men, Bonnie gave birth to her fourth child. DNA tests confirmed the baby was Blake's, and they married on November 19, 2000. It was an unusual marriage. Bakley lived in a guesthouse behind Blake's home and continued her lonely-hearts swindle, charming and robbing numerous men. (The day after her murder, Bonnie received two boxes filled with love letters and cash.) Her address book listed dozens of stars, with their yearly incomes. A "day log" detailed her letters and phone calls to celebrities, seeking new relationships.

Such activities strained Bakley's marriage to Blake in the same way it separated her from her family. Although invited by Blake, not one of Bakley's relatives attended her funeral.

TOO MANY SUSPECTS

Police investigating Bonnie Bakley's strange, often criminal lifestyle identified hundreds of enemies. Bakley herself claimed several violent encounters with the men she teased and swindled, but it never stopped her from pursuing risky pleasures.

Meanwhile, Robert Blake refused to take a polygraph (lie-detector) test on the night of the murder, saying he was too upset. He also allegedly referred to the O.J. Simpson case, saying he might fail the test because he dreamed of killing Bonnie and blamed himself for not protecting her. Simpson told reporters that he sympathized with Blake and was "pretty fascinated" by the case.

Los Angeles police commanders, still embarrassed by the Simpson trial and other scandals, assigned 17 top detectives to the Bakley murder. On May 5, officers searched Blake's home and questioned him again, then issued statements denying that Blake was a suspect. Despite that announcement, Blake hired criminal attorney Harland Braun. Detectives refused to discuss what they found in Blake's home.

Braun quickly countered media rumors of Blake's guilt by leaking information on Bonnie, including pages from her address book and tape recordings of phone conversations wherein she discussed scamming Blake and other celebrities. Braun described her as an "evil" person with countless enemies.

Police had no witness to the murder, but others cast doubt on Blake's story. The owner of the restaurant where the couple last dined denied that Blake ever returned for his gun before Bakley was shot. Employees also said that they had cleared Blake's table when he left, and found no gun.

Confusion surrounds the results of two different types of tests for gunshot residue performed by police on Blake's hands. Lawyer Braun told reporters the test results were negative, while police refused to comment. The official results—like Bakley's autopsy report—have never been released.

On May 7, 2001, officers found a Walther PPK pistol in a trash bin on Woodbridge Avenue near the spot where Blake parked his car. The gun's serial number was filed off to prevent a trace. Early reports said the pistol held three cartridges, two of which were fired, but the Walther *ejects* spent shells with each trigger pull.

The reports made no sense, but police test-fired the Walther and announced that it had killed Bonnie Bakley. They also admitted

Actor Robert Blake appears in Los Angeles Superior Court in October 2002 for a bail hearing. Blake was accused of killing his wife, Bonnie Lee Bakley. *Robert Galbraith/AP*

that cartridges left in the gun did not match those found in Blake's home. Rumors circulated that a professional hitman, hired by Blake or someone else, had committed the murder.

Eleven months after the killing, on April 18, 2002, police charged Blake with murdering his wife. They also charged his bodyguard,

Earle Caldwell, with conspiracy. Blake posted $1 million bail and was released on April 27, but a judge revoked his bond and returned Blake to jail on May 1. Ten and a half months later, on March 13, 2003, Blake was freed on $1.5 million bail pending trial.

Throughout the long investigation, Blake and Caldwell both proclaimed their innocence, describing Bakley as a woman with many enemies, who made more every day. Some of the letters aired by Braun from Bonnie's stash seemed threatening, and Caldwell described an unknown short-haired man (nicknamed "Buzz Cut") whom he saw lurking several times around Blake's home.

Police dismissed those claims as smokescreens. At a press conference held on the day of Blake's arrest, police spokesmen said Blake had killed Bonnie because "he was trapped in a marriage he wanted no part of." They spoke vaguely of "physical and significant circumstantial evidence," but gave no details. Harland Braun replied that anyone who ever met Bakley had motive to kill her.

TRIAL: ROUND ONE

As his trial slowly approached, Blake had trouble keeping lawyers. Harland Braun and Jennifer Keller both quit when Blake ignored their warnings to avoid TV interviews, and Thomas Mesereau Jr. replaced them.

Meanwhile, the tabloids had a field day. Two Hollywood stuntmen claimed that Blake had offered them money to kill his wife; one later admitted lying to police. A woman from Washington state claimed knowledge implicating Christian Brando, who dated Bakley until she married Blake—and who killed his sister's boyfriend in 1990, serving half of a 10-year prison term for manslaughter. Blake himself named Brando as a suspect in Bakley's death.

Blake and Caldwell won an early round in October 2003, when Judge Darlene Schempp dismissed their conspiracy charges, calling the prosecution's evidence "so speculative that it carries little weight." Attorney Mesereau announced that he would call 670 witnesses at trial, all supporting Blake's claim of innocence—but Mesereau also quit the case in February 2004 in the midst of jury selection.

Gerald Schwartzbach was next in line to defend Blake, with the trial postponed once again. When court finally convened in early 2005, Blake faced one charge of killing his wife and two counts of asking others to kill her. On March 16, 2005, jurors acquitted Blake of murder and one count of solicitation. They deadlocked 11-1 for acquittal on the third charge.

District Attorney Stephen Cooley branded Blake a "miserable human being" and called the jurors "incredibly stupid." Blake told

⚲ DOUBLE JEOPARDY

The U.S. Constitution's Fifth Amendment states that no person may be "twice put in jeopardy of life or limb" for the same offense—meaning that once a defendant is acquitted of a specific crime, he or she may not be tried again for that offense. Some notorious American killers have been acquitted in court, and then sold their confessions to the media.

However, as with most rules, there are loopholes.

First, *criminal* and *civil* cases are completely separate. One jury may find a defendant *not guilty* of murder, while another panel may find the same person *responsible* for wrongful death. Civil verdicts send no one to prison, but may produce heavy financial penalties.

Another loophole is the difference between *state* and *federal* charges. Most crimes like arson, murder, and robbery are tried in state court, but some also have corresponding federal jurisdiction. For example, in the 1960s, racist southern juries often freed white defendants who killed or terrorized African Americans. Federal prosecutors later jailed some of those terrorists for federal crimes such as conspiracy to violate their victims' civil rights. Today, defendants are sometimes convicted of both state *and* federal charges related to the same offense, thereby increasing their penalties.

In rare cases, prosecutors may also appeal an acquittal. That unusual step is only allowed if (a) the first trial is proved to be a fraud—as where a defendant bribes the judge or jurors to acquit him—or (b) where a judge throws out a jury's guilty verdict and acquits a defendant from the bench. In the first case, a successful appeal results in a new trial; in the second, a prosecution victory reinstates the original jury verdict without further proceedings.

courtroom reporters, "If you live to be a million, you will never ever in your life meet anyone more blessed than me."

TRIAL: ROUND TWO

Civil attorneys did not wait for Blake's acquittal to file civil charges against him. In May 2001 lawyers for Bakley's four children sued Blake and Caldwell for wrongful death, without claiming specific damages. When they questioned Caldwell, he refused to provide any answers except his name, citing the Fifth Amendment's protection against self-incrimination.

As in the earlier Simpson case, jurors ruled against Blake at trial, finding him responsible for Bakley's death on November 18, 2005. The panel ordered him to pay $30 million as a "message of deterrence"—$7.5 million for each of Bakley's children. A vote of 10-2 excused Caldwell from liability in Bakley's death.

Afterward, when reporters asked if jurors thought Blake shot his wife or hired a killer, most simply shrugged. One said, "We just don't know." Jurors *did* say they were influenced by Blake's insulting attitude toward the plaintiff's attorney, calling him "chief" and a "liar" in court.

Blake filed for bankruptcy on February 3, 2006. Soon afterward, he moved into a small apartment and announced that he was working as a ranch hand. His oldest daughter adopted Blake's baby with Bakley.

In March 2006 Blake's lawyers accused the civil jurors of misconduct, claiming that several jurors violated court instructions and that one failed to disclose that her daughter was imprisoned for murder. Jurors denied the charges, and Judge David Schacter rejected Blake's plea for a new trial.

So far, no money has been paid on the judgment or to Blake's latest attorney. On April 10, 2006, Gerald Schwartzbach told *Court TV*, "He's not paying me, and I'm not making much money representing him. [But] I don't go away. It's not over."

The Price
of Fame

Celebrities, by definition, are persons celebrated by society. They reap fame and fortune because of their talent, their appearance, or their relationship to other rich and famous people. Those fabulous rewards would not be possible without publicity—but great fame also has its price.

One risk faced by celebs is the threat of stalkers who harass—or even kill—their favorite stars (see Chapter 4). Another is the high rate of celebrity divorce. More than half of all modern American marriages fail, but the divorce rate is even higher in Hollywood, where personal relationships often wither in the spotlight.

Celebrities also fall prey to alcohol and drug abuse. Whether the rate of such abuse is worse among the rich and famous than for noncelebrities remains unclear, but when a star goes into rehab, it makes global headlines—a pressure that makes recovery that much more arduous.

PAPARAZZI PANIC

While celebrities are literally lost without media attention, some relentless photographers (dubbed *paparazzi*) behave more like stalkers than journalists. In many cases, their behavior is outrageous, including gross invasions of privacy and physical pursuit that may cause injury or loss of life.

The film *Paparazzi* (2004) examines a movie star hounded by ruthless photographers until he takes violent revenge for their

Journalists wait in the rain at Castello Odescalchi in the Italian lakeside town of Bracciano, where actors Tom Cruise and Katie Holmes were married in a star-studded ceremony, braving hordes of paparazzi. *Chris Helgren/Reuters/Corbis*

assaults on his family. While that story is fiction, real-life events keep paparazzi in the news.

Some observers blame photographers for the death of Lady Diana Spencer, former Princess of Wales, on August 31, 1997. Paparazzi in several vehicles were chasing Diana's car in Paris when it crashed at high speed, killing her and her millionaire boyfriend, Dodi Fayed. No charges were filed in Diana's death, but in February 2006 three paparazzi were fined one euro each for snapping photos of Diana as she lay dying in the wreckage.

In October 1998, California passed a law designed to limit paparazzi invasions of personal privacy. While including no criminal penalties, the law permits civil lawsuits against so-called "stalkerazzi" who snap photos on private property or use long-distance lenses to spy on private moments. If found guilty, a defendant must surrender all money earned from the sale of such photos. Seven years later, a new law tripled damages celebrities may collect if assaulted by photographers. So far, neither law has produced a court case.

Actress Reese Witherspoon complained to Los Angeles police in April 2005 after paparazzi surrounded her at her gym, but prosecutors filed no charges in that case.

Actress/singer Linsday Lohan suffered minor injuries on May 31, 2005, when a photographer allegedly rammed her car with his van. Los Angeles police jailed Galo Ramirez for suspicion of assault with a deadly weapon, then freed him on $35,000 bail.

Singer Britney Spears suffered repeated incidents with paparazzi in 2006. First, while fleeing photographers on February 7, she was caught on film driving illegally with her infant son in her lap, rather than in a car seat. Three months later, Spears tripped and nearly dropped the child on a New York sidewalk while mobbed by paparazzi.

In spring 2006, while actors Brad Pitt and Angelina Jolie awaited the birth of their first child in Namibia, leaders of that African country banned paparazzi from stalking the couple. Four who ignored that order were deported on April 25.

Heiress/actress Paris Hilton blamed paparazzi for a minor car accident on June 8, 2006, but police dismissed the incident as a case of careless parking.

EQUAL JUSTICE?

There is no question that celebrity affects the conduct of police and prosecutors, jurors and judges. In criminal cases, whether a celebrity is victim or offender, massive publicity changes everything.

We have seen how celebrity "show trials"—like those in the Blake, Lindbergh, and Simpson cases—sometimes produce strange verdicts. It is a fact that wealthy people can afford the best lawyers, and that famous defendants may sometimes charm juries.

But the reverse is also true. Winona Ryder's case suggests that she was treated more harshly than the average shoplifter in Los Angeles by prosecutors who rely on public votes to keep their jobs. Her successful appeal of the felony charges supports that suspicion.

Another strange case involves the death of comedian John Belushi (1949–1982) in Los Angeles. Belushi was a drug addict who hated needles, often asking others to inject him with cocaine or heroin. On March 5, 1982, a friend named Cathy Smith shared drugs with Belushi, resulting in Belushi's fatal overdose. Prosecutors charged Smith with first-degree murder (a planned, malicious slaying), but later accepted a plea bargain to manslaughter. Smith served 18 months in prison for an offense police probably would have ignored were it not for Belushi's "big name."

Many persons have trouble with the law throughout their lives, but never make it on TV and rarely rate a mention in the newspaper. The very opposite is true for celebrities such as actor Robert Downey Jr. and singer Courtney Love, whose every argument, traffic offense, or lapse from drug rehab generates tabloid headlines and special features on entertainment news programs.

How many noncelebrities in America could tolerate such scrutiny around the clock?

GETTING AWAY WITH MURDER?

At the other end of the spectrum, many critics say that fame and fortune help celebrities get away with murder—sometimes literally. While the Robert Blake and O.J. Simpson cases are most often cited, other celebrities also have emerged from fatal incidents without any serious penalty.

Edward "Teddy" Kennedy was elected to the U.S. Senate in 1962, while his brother, John, was President of the United States and brother, Robert, was Attorney General. On July 18, 1969, while leaving a late-night party on Chappaquiddick Island, Massachusetts, Kennedy drove off a bridge and into the water below. He escaped from the car, but left passenger Mary Jo Kopechne to drown. Kennedy later said he *tried* to save Kopechne, then swam ashore and walked to a friend's house, where he waited 10 hours before notifying police of the crash. Kennedy later pled guilty to leaving the scene of an accident, but a judge suspended his 60-day jail sentence. Kennedy remained in the U.S. Senate at press time for this book.

Claudine Longet, a popular singer and ex-wife of TV star Andy Williams, shot and killed her boyfriend, Olympic skier Vladimir "Spider" Sabich, at their Colorado home on March 21, 1976. Autopsy results showed that Sabich was shot in the back from six feet away, while blood tests on Longet revealed cocaine use. Her diary described many bitter fights with Sabich. Still, she called the shooting accidental and jurors acquitted her of manslaughter, while finding her guilty of misdemeanor negligence. She paid a small fine and served 30 days in jail, allowed to pick the days herself and stay home on weekends. The Sabich family sued Longet for wrongful death and settled out of court.

Vince Neil, former lead singer for the band Motley Crüe, was driving drunk when he crashed his car in 1984, killing passenger Nicholas "Razzle" Dingley (drummer for the band Hanoi Rocks). Neil later pled guilty to manslaughter but served only 30 days in jail.

Rebecca Gayheart, star of films and television, struck and killed a nine-year-old jaywalker while driving through Hollywood on June 13, 2001. At the time of the accident, she was driving 40 miles per hour in a 25-mph zone, while passing several cars that had stopped to let the boy cross Bronson Avenue. Gayheart pled no contest to misdemeanor vehicular manslaughter, receiving a one-year suspension of her driver's license, three years probation, a $2,800 fine, and 750 hours of community service (making TV commercials on traffic safety). The victim's parents sued for wrongful death. Gayheart settled out of court in 2002 for an undisclosed amount.

ENDURING MYSTERIES

While some celebrity cases provoke laughter, and others outrage, a few—like the death of Bob Crane—remain as haunting mysteries and the subjects of dramatic conspiracy theories. Puzzles surrounding a celebrity death can enhance that person's posthumous fame, but they also raise the question of whether or not celebrity status can actually interfere with the course of justice for some victims. Although these cases may be officially closed, alternate theories keep them open in the public consciousness.

William Desmond Taylor was the star of 25 films and director of 67 more between 1913 and 1921. On February 1, 1922, an employee found Taylor shot dead in his Los Angeles home. Suspects included two famous actresses, a starlet's mother, a neighbor, Taylor's butler, and his own brother, but no charges were ever filed.

Paul Bern, a director and screenwriter, was married to movie star Jean Harlow. Bern was found nude and shot through the head at the couple's Beverly Hills home on September 5, 1932. A note beside his body read: "Last night was only a comedy." While police ruled the death suicide, various authors claim it was murder.

FATTY ARBUCKLE: BLACKMAIL VICTIM

Because of their wealth and status, celebrities sometimes draw the attention of criminals, who see them as ready-made victims willing to pay any amount to protect their public image. The price of refusal can be high.

Roscoe "Fatty" Arbuckle (1887–1933) was a silent film star who made 154 comic movies between 1909 and 1921. On September 5, 1921, he hosted a party in his suite at San Francisco's St. Francis Hotel with two male friends and several young women. During the party 26-year-old starlet Virginia Rappe became ill, but the hotel's doctor said that she was simply drunk. In fact, Rappe had a disease that made her violently sick when she drank alcohol. She died three days later from infection caused by a ruptured bladder.

Maude Delmont, Rappe's friend, tried to blackmail Arbuckle, demanding money to suppress her claim that he injured Rappe while trying to rape her. Arbuckle refused to pay, so Delmont told her story to police. Newspapers turned the accusation into a major scandal, harping on the theme of "a fat man's foulness." A prosecutor with dreams of becoming governor charged Arbuckle with rape and murder on September 17.

Suspects named in print include MGM Vice President Eddie Mannix, Dorothy Millette (Bern's former lover, who killed herself the day after his death), and New Jersey gangster Abner "Longy" Zwillman (allegedly Harlow's lover). Harlow died in June 1937, without speaking publicly about the incident.

Marilyn Monroe, Hollywood's "blond bombshell" and star of 32 films, died at her Los Angeles home on the night of August 4, 1962. Medical examiners blamed her death on a drug overdose, either accidental or deliberate. Various independent investigators believe Monroe was murdered to stop her from revealing guilty secrets learned during her love affairs with President John Kennedy and his brother, Attorney General Robert Kennedy.

Jim Morrison, lead singer for the rock band the Doors during the late 1960s and early 1970s, moved to Paris in March 1971 and apparently died there four months later, on July 3. No autopsy was performed, leaving the cause of death unclear, though some authors

Those charges were later reduced to manslaughter. Arbuckle faced trial three times between November 1921 and March 1922. Two juries deadlocked without reaching verdicts. The third jury acquitted Arbuckle and issued a public statement saying: "Acquittal is not enough for Roscoe Arbuckle. We feel that a great injustice has been done him."

Still, many in Hollywood treated Arbuckle as if he was guilty. Movie censor Will Hays banned Arbuckle from making films in April 1922, and then changed his mind eight months later. Arbuckle made 10 more films between 1922 and 1933, but they were poorly attended and most are now lost.

The scandal also affected Arbuckle's personal life. His wife stood by him through the trials, despite a stalker's attempt to kill her, but the couple divorced in January 1925. Arbuckle married twice more, in 1925 and 1931, but he never seemed truly happy. When he died in June 1933, at age 46, friend and comedian Buster Keaton blamed a broken heart—the price of fame in Hollywood.

suspect a drug overdose. Other researchers and dedicated fans insist that Morrison faked his own death to escape the celebrity rat race and lives on today under another name.

John Lennon was definitely shot by Mark David Chapman in 1980. Still, speculation continues regarding Chapman's true motives. Author Fenton Bresler, in his book *Who Killed John Lennon?* (1989), blames the Central Intelligence Agency for Lennon's murder, claiming that Lennon's opposition to war threatened America's aggressive foreign policy.

Kurt Cobain, lead singer for the grunge band Nirvana, apparently shot himself in April 1994 after a long struggle with heroin addiction. Despite an official suicide ruling, several authors insist that Cobain was murdered. Most conspiracy theorists accuse Cobain's wife, singer Courtney Love, of plotting his death. So far, the only "evidence" of murder is an unsubstantiated claim by punk rock singer El Duce that Love offered him $50,000 to kill Cobain. Love denies all such claims, but has not sued the various authors for libel.

Chronology

1593 *March* **England:** Famed playwright Christopher Marlowe is fatally stabbed in a tavern. His killer successfully pleads self-defense.

1906 *June* **New York City:** Millionaire Harry Thaw fatally shoots celebrity architect Stanford White.

1919 *October* **Chicago:** Eight players on the Chicago White Sox accept bribes to lose the World Series, earning their team the nickname "Chicago Black Sox."

1921 *September* **Los Angeles:** Police charge comic actor Roscoe "Fatty" Arbuckle with killing starlet Virginia Rappe. Jurors acquit Arbuckle in 1923.

1922 *February* **Los Angeles:** Actor-director William Desmond Taylor is fatally shot at his home. The case remains unsolved.

1926 *May* **California:** Evangelist Aime Semple McPherson stages a fake kidnapping, surfacing in Mexico a month later.

1958 *March* **Los Angeles:** Cheryl Crane, daughter of movie star Lana Turner, fatally stabs Turner's gangster boyfriend, Johnny Stompanato.

1959 *January* **California:** Carl "Alfalfa" Switzer, star of the *Our Gang* comedy series, is fatally shot while arguing with a friend.

1961 *April* **Los Angeles:** Country singer Spade Cooley murders his wife.

1962 *August* **Los Angeles:** Screen star Marilyn Monroe dies from a drug overdose at her home. Despite an official suicide verdict, theories of murder persist.

1963 *December* **Lake Tahoe, Nev.:** Kidnappers hold Frank Sinatra Jr. for ransom, releasing him on payment of $240,000.

1964 *December* **Los Angeles:** A hotel manager shoots singer Sam Cooke. Police rule the killing self-defense.

1969   *August*   ***Los Angeles:*** Members of Charles Manson's gang kill seven persons, including actress Sharon Tate.

1976   *February*   ***Hollywood:*** Actor Sal Mineo dies from stab wounds. Jurors convict his killer in March 1979.

   March   ***California:*** Singer Claudine Longet fatally shoots her boyfriend, Olympic skier Spider Sabich.

1978   *June*   ***Scottsdale, Ariz.:*** TV star Bob Crane is fatally beaten at his home.

   October   ***New York City:*** Nancy Spungen suffers fatal stab wounds in a hotel room shared with her boyfriend, punk rocker Sid Vicious. The case remains officially unsolved.

1980   *December*   ***New York City:*** Stalker Mark Chapman murders musician John Lennon.

1981   *March*   ***Washington, D.C.:*** John Hinckley Jr. shoots President Ronald Reagan in hopes of impressing actress Jodie Foster.

1982   *March*   ***Los Angeles:*** A religious-fanatic stalker stabs actress Theresa Saldana, who starred in *Raging Bull* (1980).

1984   *March*   ***Los Angeles:*** Soul singer Marvin Gaye Jr. is fatally shot by his father.

1989   *July*   ***Hollywood:*** A stalker murders actress Rebecca Schaeffer.

1990   *May*   ***Los Angeles:*** Christian Brando, son of actor Marlon Brando, kills his sister's boyfriend. He is later convicted of voluntary manslaughter.

1992   *February*   World heavyweight boxing champion Mike Tyson is convicted of a rape that occurred the previous year and sentenced to six years in prison; he serves three.

1993   *August*   ***Los Angeles:*** Police charge rapper "Snoop Dogg" with murder. Jurors acquit him based on evidence that his bodyguard fired the fatal shots.

1994   *June*   ***Los Angeles:*** Police accuse athlete-actor O.J. Simpson of killing his ex-wife and a male friend. Jurors acquit Simpson of murder in October 1994. A civil jury awards survivors $8.5 million in February 1997.

1996 *September Las Vegas:* Rap star Tupac Shakur suffers fatal gunshot wounds shortly after brawling with members of the Crips street gang.

1996 *November California:* Actor Robert Downey Jr. receives a three-year prison term on drug and weapons charges. Upon release, he violates parole and returns to prison in August 1999. Two more drug arrests follow, in November 2000 and April 2001.

1997 *March Los Angeles:* Gunmen kill rapper the Notorious B.I.G., a rival of Tupac Shakur.

2001 *May Los Angeles:* Police charge actor Robert Blake with killing his wife, Bonnie Lee Bakley. Jurors acquit him of murder in March 2005. A civil jury finds him liable in November 2005, ordering payment of $30 million to Bakley's family.

2002 *January New Orleans:* Rapper C Murder fatally shoots an underage fan at the Platinum Club. Convicted in October 2002, he successfully appeals for a new trial in March 2006.

February Pakistan: American actor Erik Audé is imprisoned for smuggling opium. He was freed in 2004 following the confession of an Armenian man who duped him into transporting the drugs.

2003 *August* Popular Los Angeles Lakers star Kobe Bryant is accused of sexual assault in a case that mars his clean public image; the charges were eventually dropped.

2005 *June Los Angeles:* Jurors acquit singer Michael Jackson of child molestation charges.

2007 *August Atlanta:* Falcons quarterback Michael Vick pleads guilty to charges involving illegal dog fighting and accepts a prison sentence.

September The trial of star record producer Phil Spector for the murder of Lana Clarkson ends in a hung jury; a new trial was not yet scheduled at this writing.

Endnotes

Chapter 1

1. Ludovic Kennedy, *Crime of the Century* (New York: Penguin Books, 1996), 281.

Chapter 2

1. Death Penalty Information Center, "Executions in the U.S. 1608–2002," http://www.deathpenaltyinfo.org/ESPYyear.pdf (accessed January 10, 2008).
2. Clark County (Ind.) Prosecuting Attorney. "The Death Penalty," http://www.clarkprosecutor.org/html/death/dpusa.htm.

Chapter 5

1. Smith, Philip. "Star Scams: Celebrity Con Man," Sunday Mirror, http://findarticles.com/p/articles/mi_qn4161/Is_20021201/ai_n12857813 (accessed January 14, 2008).
2. Gimbel, Barney. "A Tarnished Celebrity Moneyman's New Scam," CNNMoney.com. http://money.cnn.com/magazines/fortune/fortune_archive/2006/10/16/8388684/index.htm (accessed January 14, 2008).

Chapter 6

1. Vincent Bugliosi, *Outrage: The Five Reasons O.J. Simpson Got Away With Murder* (New York: Island Books, 1997), pp. 180–193.

Bibliography

Bugliosi, Vincent. *Outrage: The Five Reasons Why O.J. Simpson Got Away With Murder*. New York: Island Books, 1997.

Bugliosi, Vincent, and Curt Gentry. *Helter Skelter*. New York: W.W. Norton, 1974.

Crockett, Art, ed. *Celebrity Murders*. New York: Pinnacle, 1990.

Edwards, Mona, and Jody Handley. *Captured!: Inside the World of Celebrity Trials*. Santa Monica, Calif.: Santa Monica Press, 2006.

Graysmith, Robert. *The Murder Of Bob Crane*. New York: Crown, 1993.

Harvey, Davie. *Obsession: Celebrities and Their Stalkers*. Dublin: Merlin, 2003.

Kennedy, Ludovic. *The Airman and the Carpenter*. New York: Viking, 1985.

King, Gary. *Murder In Hollywood*. New York: St. Martin's Paperbacks, 2001.

Meloy, J. Reid, ed. *The Psychology of Stalking*. San Diego: Academic Press, 1998.

Sanders, Ed. *The Family*. New York: Thunder's Mouth Press, 2002.

Sauerwein, Stan. *Celebrity Stalkers*. Canmore, Alberta: Altitude, 2006.

Scott, Cathy. *The Killing of Tupac Shakur*. Las Vegas: Huntington Press, 2002.

Shepard, Charles. *Forgiven: The Rise and Fall of Jim Bakker and the PTL Ministry*. New York: Atlantic Monthly Press, 1989.

Sullivan, Randall. *Labyrinth*. New York: Grove Press, 2003.

Time-Life Books. *True Crime: Death and Celebrity*. New York: Time-Life UK, 2004.

Further Resources

Books

Ellis, Chris, and Julie Ellis. *The Mammoth Book of Celebrity Murder*. New York: Carroll & Graf, 2005.

Olsen, Marilyn. *Arrested!: Celebrities Caught in the Act*. Long Island City, N.Y.: Hatherleigh Press, 2003.

Sifakis, Carl. *Crimes and the Rich and Famous*. New York: Checkmark Books, 2001.

Online

Arresting Images (celebrity mugshots)
http://www.thesmokinggun.com/mugshots/index.html#theLinks

Crime Library
http://www.crimelibrary.com

People in Hot Water (news about crime and celebrities)
http://www.showbuzz.cbsnews.com/sections/people_hot_water/main500656.shtml

Index

Page numbers in *italics* indicate images.

About the Author

A former public school teacher (grades 6–8, 1979–86), Michael Newton has published 202 books since 1977, with 12 more scheduled for release from various houses through 2010. His first nonfiction book—*Monsters, Mysteries and Man* (Addison-Wesley, 1979)—was a volume for young readers on cryptozoology and UFOs. His recent reference works include *The Encyclopedia of Serial Killers* (2d edition, 2006) and seven other books from Facts on File (2000–07), plus the *FBI Encyclopedia* and an *Encyclopedia of Cryptozoology* (McFarland, 2004 and 2005). His history of the Florida Ku Klux Klan, *The Invisible Empire* (University Press of Florida, 2001), won the Florida Historical Society's 2002 Rembert Patrick Award for Best Book on Florida History. A full list of Newton's published and forthcoming titles may be found on his Web site at http://www.michaelnewton.homestead.com.

About the Consulting Editor

John L. French is a 31-year veteran of the Baltimore City Police Crime Laboratory. He is currently a crime laboratory supervisor. His responsibilities include responding to crime scenes, overseeing the preservation and collection of evidence, and training crime scene technicians. He has been actively involved in writing the operating procedures and technical manual for his unit and has conducted training in numerous areas of crime scene investigation. In addition to his crime scene work, Mr. French is also a published author, specializing in crime fiction. His short stories have appeared in *Alfred Hitchcock's Mystery Magazine* and numerous anthologies.